SYRUP SANDWICHES

Choose Not to Give Up!

SYRUP SANDWICHES

Choose Not to Give Up!

Anthony Owens

Anchor Book Press • Palatine

Syrup Sandwiches: Choose Not to Give Up!
Copyright © Anthony Owens 2022
Cover Design by Robert J. Fluegel
Photography by James D. Moore
Anchor Book Press, Ltd
440 W Colfax Street, Unit 1132, Palatine, IL 60078
ISBN: 978-1949109955
Library of Congress Control Number: 2022945550

Printed in the United States

All rights reserved. No part of this publication may be reproduced, stored in a retrieval system, or transmitted in any form by any means, except for brief quotations, without the prior written permission of the author.

Dedication

I dedicate this book to my Aunt Lillie, who passed away due to complications of Alzheimer's disease at the age of seventy-two. I am thankful and fortunate to have had her in my life, and she will be truly missed.

Acknowledgements

I am thankful and appreciative to all those who have joined me on this journey. I especially want to thank Jane Kennedy Mitchell for helping me develop my writing structure and flow to better present my ideas. She provided invaluable insight into character and plot development. I also thank Elizabeth Yeamans Simrell for her expert editorial proofreading, copyediting, and content development. I thank Nicole Owens for her initial editing efforts and assistance. I greatly appreciate Carol Pirog for her insightful vision and illuminating the relevance of *Syrup Sandwiches*. To my family and friends who have supported me throughout this lengthy process, I greatly appreciate their encouragement, even when the long hours of writing interfered with our socializing. A special thanks to my granddaughter, Billie, who has shown me that I'm not too old to learn new things, and to finally appreciate and enjoy life.

Table of Contents

Chapter 1 - Now and Later 3

Chapter 2 - The Lord's Day 12

Chapter 3 - Grandparents 28

Chapter 4 - Time for a Change 39

Chapter 5 - Greg 48

Chapter 6 - Syrup Sandwiches 53

Chapter 7 - A Better Place 58

Chapter 8 - Fire Escape 67

Chapter 9 - Pitkin Avenue 78

Chapter 10 - Trendsetter 86

Chapter 11 - Blackout 93

Chapter 12 - Bullies 103

Chapter 13 - Summer Job 109

Chapter 14 - Brownstone 115

Chapter 15 - Gainfully Employed 120

Chapter 16 - Career Day 126

Chapter 17 - Sweet Goodbyes 134

Chapter 18 - Navy Life 140

Chapter 19 - Husband Then Father 150

Chapter 20 - Searching for My Father 158

Chapter 21 - Sunny Florida 170

Chapter 22 - Back to Virginia 179

Chapter 23 - Get Out 187

Chapter 24 - Bye-bye, Navy 192

Chapter 25 - Foster Parent 198
Chapter 26 - Cookout 206
Chapter 27 - More Poor Decisions 213
Chapter 28 - Big Brother 218
Chapter 29 - Pain in the Neck 225
Chapter 30 - A New Birth 228

Foreword

Syrup Sandwiches is an inspiring book which highlights the resiliency and determination of the human spirit to succeed. The author, Anthony Owens, spent his childhood living in poverty and experiencing trauma. Many educators will agree with what the data reveals; children like Anthony too often cannot find success in the educational environment. As an educator and trauma specialist, I've spent nearly 20 years working my hardest to prove that data doesn't have to be true. Whether children come from poverty or have experienced trauma, they still long for success, although it seems beyond their reach. Year after year, however, it seems that some of those children fight to flourish, despite the obstacles in their way or the lack of adult support. *Syrup Sandwiches* give us insight into the personal characteristics of the students, like Anthony, who succeed.

Anthony Owens' story takes his readers on an in-depth journey of what it takes to succeed against the odds. Yes, it's a great read for young men and women who are desperately looking for guidance and heartfelt stories of success. This book also provides us, the adults, with a firsthand account of what is needed to help children find a way to succeed, even when it seems unattainable. As an educator reading *Syrup Sandwiches*, I was reminded of a quote by Horace Mann, "Education is the great equalizer." Seeing the graduation rates at Anthony's high school in *Syrup Sandwiches*, I found myself searching through the pages of *Syrup Sandwiches* for answers to my questions: "Why is Anthony Owens, a poor, fatherless, black boy, a successful man today? What experiences and mindset did young Anthony possess that most of the students at his high school lacked? What personal traits gave him the intrinsic determination to push forward when others quit? What was it that helped Anthony become the successful husband and father he is today?" Not only did Anthony graduate high school, but he also earned a master's degree!

Horace Mann's principle should be the foundation for every child's educational experience. While an education won't guarantee success in and by itself, the lack of an education does result in failure in the economic arena of employment. Anthony Owen's *Syrup Sandwiches* also highlights other qualities that are necessary beyond an education, but an education is the foundation. In my book, *Can You See Me,* I also provide insight into the core concepts that help low-income students 'buy' into education. These concepts might sound like common sense to many, but are often overlooked, such as Anthony's relationship with his teacher and being held accountable when his mother insisted the boys finish their homework before joining their friends. Because, in addition to education, relationships and accountability are critical, too.

Syrup Sandwiches was released at a time when the world is looking for answers. I believe that Anthony has the answers for long-lasting success for all children, especially children of color who have experienced trauma and poverty. Anthony shows us it is possible to be a victim of poverty and trauma without being defeated. He shows us through his story that it is possible to beat the odds by refusing to embrace the victim mindset, to prevail when the environment is working against you and society is saying you can't. Our responsibility is to the children of today. Our responsibility is to create hope in the lives of the children in our world. Together, we can create a world where all can succeed. *Syrup Sandwiches* is a must read for all adults who need insight into the black experience and the trauma experience in order to facilitate hope for the children who live with that reality every day.

Belinda Adams
Author, Educator, and Trauma Specialist

I am what time, circumstances, and history have made of me, certainly, but I am also much more than that. So are we all.
                                    James Baldwin

So, I Begin
A Note to the Reader

As a boy in Brooklyn, I would often ask my mother about my father and his family, and she would say she didn't know where they were or how to get in touch with them. My brother was in the same boat. I guessed that our fathers were still back in Georgia, where we came from, and that they didn't care about us.

My dad wasn't around, but growing up, James and I were subjected to several *father figures*. We shared a maternal grandfather. We knew my mother's brothers who lived in Brooklyn. And we got to know my mother's boyfriend, Greg.

However, I didn't respect any of these men—all of them were abusive. Even as a child, I felt that my grandfather, uncles, mother's boyfriend—or any man for that matter—who chose to abuse a woman could go straight to hell.

Few men I knew had anything going for them. They were emotionally empty. They were void of compassion and common sense. James and I quickly learned not to expect anything from them—not money, not time, not advice, not guidance, and certainly not love.

The problem with my uncles was that they all shared the same father. My grandfather did nothing to comfort or provide for any of his children; needless to say, neither did his sons. And, as a child, hearing the sad family stories, I became determined not to be like my grandfather or any of the other men in my life. But living up to the ideal man I wanted to be wasn't easy.

Without positive male role models, how did James and I get direction, support, or even plain old advice on how to be a man? Mostly, from each other.

Left to watch these irresponsible men, we had to figure out what *not* to do. We had to become clever and hardworking ourselves to fill the gaping holes in our lives. We had to become strong and quick to handle a string of life-threatening crises. So, that's what we did.

Thankfully for my brother and me, there was one caring parent—our mother. Although she didn't always make the best decisions, she loved us. And she wanted us to grow up to be better than the men she knew in her life. The emotional support and endurance of my mother emboldened me to struggle with the rough circumstances of my growing-up years. Her concern for us encouraged me to counter the negative male role models of my life and to take on some of the responsibilities of caring for my brother and myself, and later, our little sister.

And there was another inspiring source of support for our family, my mother's sister, Aunt Lillie. A talented and resourceful woman, she made clothes that not only fit me but ones I wanted to wear. She had challenges in her life, but she met them with pluck and energy. She taught me to never give up even when it seems like the world isn't going to change in my favor.

The chapters ahead don't describe a trek up the tallest mountain or a cure for a mysterious disease. They show how the course of one man's life was changed and how that change affected others. It's the story of a poor boy from Brooklyn who not only survives but succeeds at what he longs for most. Believing in the power of personal change, he becomes a devoted husband and a father who cares.

Chapter 1
Now and Later

As two hungry, growing boys in Brooklyn with time on our hands, my brother James and I had to find our own fun. I was eight and my brother was six when my mother moved us from our aunt and uncle's home in Bedford-Stuyvesant to our own apartment on the north edge of Bushwick. There we spent most of the 70s talking on the fire escape, located on the front of our building. We'd watch the J trains fly by at eye level and the bustle of Broadway Avenue below.

This was not the famous Broadway of Manhattan. Yet, from our metal seats on the top floor, we heard yelling, arguing, and cursing that, as kids, we found entertaining. It was amazing how sound carried from the street up four stories. People on ground level sounded as if they were in our kitchen. When drivers stopped blasting their horns—impatient drivers would honk steadily for what seemed to us like hours—we could even overhear intimate conversations that would have otherwise remained private at ground level. Then there were the trains. When the J trains roared and rattled past, our whole building would shake, and our fire escape felt like it might fall apart.

As raucous as it could get out there, it was more comfortable for me and James out on the fire escape than being cooped up inside. We'd stay outside at our private getaway, even on cold days when the radiators clanked to warm the apartment. The fire escape was our balcony.

One of those old-fashioned steam radiators stood under the window that opened to the fire escape. Whenever I see a silver cast-iron radiator like that, I think of the fire escape ritual my brother and I practiced during cold weather. All it required was our favorite flavors of Now and Later candy and a radiator.

After removing the outside wrappers, we would reach inside the window to lay the individually wrapped Now and Later squares on the hot radiator. We'd watch the bright squares closely, letting them melt just enough. Then we'd strip away every bit of the colorful paper and stretch the gooey pieces into long, fruity strands. This was our own fire escape version of the fancy saltwater taffy we couldn't afford.

My only memory of eating the real stuff was when my Aunt Lillie came to visit us one summer after she'd been to the beach. She gave each of us two pieces, saying, "Enjoy your taffy."

The taffy was individually wrapped like the Now and Later candies, but the pieces were round and pale. We knew saltwater taffy had to be expensive because the satiny box pictured white children playing on the beach. We bit into what we thought would be the best-tasting candy in the world. As we continued to chew, we tried not to let our aunt see the disappointment on our faces. We hugged her and said, "Thank you, Auntie," then slunk outside to talk truth about this famous candy.

"What's so good about taffy?" James asked.

"Nothing, it's just chewy candy." I replied. "Guess it's all you can buy at the beach."

James and I were now completely convinced that our neighborhood candies were good enough for us. Now and Later candy was Brooklyn made, which made it extra special. As long as we had enough money, any candy would put fun into our day. And we loved that corner stores had so many choices: Boston Baked Beans,

Syrup Sandwiches

Lemonhead, Charleston Chew, Chick-O-Stick, and Oh Henry! And, of course, Now and Later. At the counter, we had fun looking over the selection and figuring out what we could buy with the change our mother had given us.

I'll never forget the last time we walked to our favorite corner store to buy candy. It was eight o'clock on a cold November night. I was thirteen and James was eleven. We'd lived on Broadway Avenue for five years, so we were allowed to go out after dark if we went together and made it quick. Our mother warned us every time that dangerous criminals walked the streets of Bushwick at night. Under our breaths we'd respond, "yeah, yeah," but we really didn't want to stay out too late—we knew how dangerous Bushwick was.

On that November evening, James wanted some more Now and Later to melt.

"I have to have me a Chick-O-Stick," I insisted. The salty peanut and coconut flavors seemed more substantial.

The store was a block away, and the trip was an adventure. All day and night the block stayed alive with cars, trucks, trains, and crowds of people. Since Bushwick was paved over and packed with buildings, I would have never imagined it as the *heavy woods* its name means. But it was woods in 1638 when the Dutch settlers bought it, fairly or not, from the Native American Canarsie tribe. In the 19th century, Bushwick became a mecca for German and Austrian brewers. Schaefer, Piels, and Rheingold made Bushwick the Beer Capital of the Northeast. Then in the early 20th century, Italians moved in, many buying their own homes. By the time we lived in Bushwick, it was a mostly Puerto Rican neighborhood with a growing number of blacks from the South like us.

It helped that we spent so much time on the fire escape watching our neighbors come and go. When we walked down the street, we could recognize almost everyone who lived on the block. Of course, because only eight families lived in our building, we knew them all by name.

On warmer evenings, we usually had to maneuver around salsa dancers, young and old, swaying back and forth on the sidewalk. Although I couldn't speak much Spanish, I learned enough to understand the small talk, numbers, and, of course, some of the bad words they used if we bumped into them. On this cold evening, there were no dancers, but we could hear the Latin music through windows and R&B from passing cars. Most people on the sidewalk were huddled up in coats and hurrying to get back inside. James and I didn't have any heavy coats, so we were wearing extra sweaters and knock-off Members Only jackets to keep us warm. We saw Ms. Rodriguez briskly walking back toward our building. She lived on the second floor.

We spoke in unison, "Hello, Ms. Rodriguez."

She responded in a heavy Hispanic accent, "Aren't you boys cold?" as she hurried past us.

We both turned around and said, "No." We were so used to the cold that it didn't bother us too much.

The store, or *bodega*, as we usually called it, was named Ruiz Deli. Picturing its classic look, I would bet it had opened way back in the 1930s. Like other Brooklyn bodegas, it had boxes and cans of food, toiletries, beer, wine, soft drinks, sandwiches, and a variety of candy.

I enjoyed going to Ruiz's. I loved the smell of the freshly brewed coffee that greeted you at the door. I loved the welcoming scent of Mr. Ruiz's Old Spice cologne. As soon as he saw me, he would say, "Hey, tall

Syrup Sandwiches

guy," in his deep accented voice. He knew my name but never used it.

Mr. Ruiz was in his late fifties. He had immigrated from Puerto Rico with his family as a young man. Standing about five five, he looked like he weighed 250 pounds. His oval bald spot shined so I could see the ceiling lights reflected on it. He had chubby cheeks and loved to smile.

When James and I walked into the store that November night, Mr. Ruiz said to Mateo, the high school kid who made hero sandwiches, "Here comes the tall guy." Mateo was also Hispanic, and often he and Mr. Ruiz would be speaking in Spanish when we walked into the store. Mateo was friendly but not like Mr. Ruiz. Mateo was usually quiet, and I think that was because his English wasn't as strong as Mr. Ruiz's.

"Hello, Mr. Ruiz," I said, trying to sound like an adult. "Can I have two Chick-O-Sticks and a pack of grape Now and Later?"

"Anything for my tall friend," he said.

The store had customers coming and going continuously, and it seemed as if Mr. Ruiz knew everyone. He addressed each customer amiably when they came in and again when they left. I can still hear his deep voice saying, "Hola, Mary. Hola, Hector; Gracias, mi amigo; Thank you, my friend;" and "Goodbye, my tall friend. Watch out for little brother. He's catching up to you."

Mr. Ruiz's upbeat attitude and friendliness made me feel at home in his store. Of all the corner stores in the neighborhood, James and I enjoyed his the most. We felt lucky it was on our block.

After our goodbyes to Mr. Ruiz, James and I paused right outside under the light of the bodega sign and tore open our candy. We were already hungry when we left home, and the cold had made us even hungrier.

"Aren't you going to save some to melt on the radiator?" I asked James.

"Nope," he said with a purple mouth full of sticky Now and Later.

We joked about the ridiculous Now and Later tagline: "Eat some now, save some for later." No one could resist eating it all at once.

We were still chewing and laughing when two loud bangs from inside jolted us. Immediately, two masked men ran out of Ruiz's, one holding a gun, the other, a paper bag. They charged straight at us, and we tumbled out of their way.

Then someone staggered from the store.

It was Mateo. Blood covered his clothes. His mouth formed a scream, but his voice came out a whisper. His eyes begged us. Mateo needed us to hear him. We made out the words, "They shot us," before he collapsed on the sidewalk.

James burst into tears. Someone shouted, "Call the police. Call the police!"

People showed up from all directions. A woman stooped to help Mateo, and a few men ran into the store. From inside, I heard someone cry out, "Mr. Ruiz is dead. He's dead. He's dead!"

My eyes teared up, and my heart pounded faster and faster. Because I couldn't believe what was going on, my physical reaction scared me. It was as if my body grasped a frightening reality my mind couldn't accept. I wanted to stay to help Mateo, but my shaking body ran. James and I ran all the way back home, crying like little kids. As the sounds of sirens blared down the street, we bolted up our building's stairs and locked the door behind us. We were no longer the same boys who had run out for a treat.

Syrup Sandwiches

After we sobbed out our story to our mother, she sat silent and motionless. She, too, had been fond of Mr. Ruiz. We gathered that the news of his death stunned her.

When our mother heard our voices in the middle of the night, she found us talking about the shooting and how we were hoping that Mateo would be OK.

My mother then said prayers for Mr. Ruiz's wife, his sons, and daughters—and Mateo.

The next day from our fire escape, we heard neighbors talking, saw them gesturing about the shooting. We soon learned that both Mr. Ruiz and Mateo had died. Mr. Ruiz never left the store alive, and Mateo had died at the hospital.

The neighborhood wasn't the same after the shooting and the closing down of Ruiz Deli. I couldn't process the scene that played over and over in my mind. Why would someone kill another person, especially someone who was friendly and kind to everyone? I started thinking that life was cruel. How could God let this happen?

For a long time afterward, James and I had nightmares. We took turns. One night, he would wake up screaming. The next night, I'd rage in the dark. We dreamed the masked killers were coming up the steps to get us. We were too old to run to our mother's bed for comfort, but the first week, our mother would come in to see if we were OK. She'd say, "How y'all doing in here?" as she entered the room. Our answer was always, "Fine," even if we weren't.

For years she had worked an exhausting job as a home attendant and had already gotten used to sleeping through loud trains. So, after weeks of hearing cries from the next room, she stopped coming in.

Word had gotten to our church about the bodega murders, and the pastor said a few kind words about Mr.

Ruiz and Mateo during the following Sunday service. He mentioned how he, too, had gone to Ruiz Deli on several occasions. I don't recall anyone from the church offering James and me counseling or even approaching us to talk about it. But I doubt anyone at New Foundation Baptist Cathedral would have been aware we had witnessed the crime. James and I didn't tell anyone but our mother. We were too afraid because the killers were at large. They might be asking neighbors if they knew boys who looked like us. We talked about going to the police, but we didn't see the point. What could we say about masked killers tearing by us under the dim light of the bodega sign?

As we pitched into December, I was still facing emotional turmoil that, at thirteen, I wasn't equipped to handle. James and I both needed someone to tell how much pain we were in. But there was no one. Sure, our mother was right there, but she was as emotionally fragile as we were. Hell, we all needed help.

After Ruiz Deli closed, James and I went to other corner stores, but it wasn't the same. Not only were the stores blocks away, but the owners and employees were unfriendly. They didn't joke around with us. They didn't know our names. They never even said hello or goodbye. They would just glare at us as if they thought we might steal something.

Arabic-speaking immigrants owned the other corner stores we tried. At first, I thought, they were new to America and couldn't speak English. But no. We overheard them speaking English. What they lacked was the language of warmth and charm that Mr. Ruiz spoke.

James and I were nervous and more cautious about going out after the shooting, especially since the police seemed to have given up on finding the killers.

Syrup Sandwiches

Our conversations on the fire escape became more serious, and we often monitored comings and goings on the street in silence. When we did go out, we planned strategically how to look out for each other. It wasn't normal. But two kindhearted neighbors had been shot just minutes after we'd said goodbye to them. How could things be normal after that?

Eating candy on the fire escape had lost its fun. We no longer did our Now and Later ritual as much. James would randomly cry, and his grief made me feel worse. All I could do was hug him and say something like, "It will be OK. Mr. Ruiz is in a better place." I didn't know if it was true, but every adult that I knew repeated that line every time someone died. It didn't matter who it was or how they'd died. They all were somehow in a better place. If rotten men and mean women ended up in a better place, Mr. Ruiz and Mateo must be in a really special place. At least that's what I hoped and what I said over and over to James.

You might think that after such a traumatic happening in the neighborhood, the community would come together to make things better. But, as far as I saw, that was not the case. If anybody had tried, then it wasn't effective. Two months after the robbery and murder at Ruiz's, there was another robbery. This time at a nearby drug store. Thank goodness, James and I weren't there.

Chapter 2
The Lord's Day

The sun had yet to rise, and neither had I, when I would hear my mother's voice, "If you don't get up and put your clothes on, I'll whip your little butt. Don't be taking all day. It's Sunday and I'm not going to be late for church."

My mother never forgot the spiritual upbringing she'd gotten in Georgia. Sister Owens, as she was called in church, would rather go without food than be late for Sunday services. Whenever my mother went to church, my brother and I went too, walking the eight blocks from our apartment. The way to church is imprinted on my mind: the junior high school, a city park, three corner stores, followed by apartment building after apartment building. James and I would end up far ahead of our mother, not because we were in any hurry to get to church but because she preferred a relaxed stroll on Sunday.

Since my mother was an usher for the church, she wore a white uniform with white orthopedic-looking shoes. She looked like a nurse. Even the hat looked like a boxy old-fashioned nurse's cap. The church ushers paid for their own uniforms as well as sets of different colored accessories that they were required to change from week to week. My young churchgoing mother comes into mental focus for me: It was a blue-sky morning, and she is wearing sky blue gloves with a blue

Syrup Sandwiches

carnation pinned to her uniform and a blue hat. Nearly slipping while wearing my loose, black Salvation Army shoes, I stopped suddenly and looked back at her to see if she'd noticed my near fall. She was gesturing to my little brother, whose white shirt was hanging below his jacket.

"Tuck that in, James!" I heard her say. "And, Anthony, don't scuff your new shoes."

Our mother made sure that James and I dressed neatly for church. We wore the best black suits and white shirts she could afford from the Salvation Army. I remember ironing my white shirt myself one Saturday night for the first time with my mother, who was at that time still taller than I, standing over me and making sure that I was doing it right.

We regularly showed up to church by seven A.M. for Sunday school. Sunday school was for me like T-ball, a place to learn the basics. My mother had already taught me how to pray: "Get down on your knees by the bed and put your hands together." And I prayed that way every night. But Sunday school taught me the kids' version of the Bible and gave me the building blocks to become a better person.

Sunday school was about as much fun as a child could expect to have in church. There were about twelve of us in the class, and for years we had the same brave teacher, Sister Edwards. Our lessons usually lasted until about eight-thirty—unless Sister Edwards had a longer conversation with the Lord the night before and wanted to share every detail. Sister Edwards started her lesson off as usual with, "The Lord loves us all, I love all of you, and I love this church."

I knew that Sister Edwards loved us and loved the church. Why else would she get up so early to spend time with a dozen rowdy kids? But I wrestled with her first words, "The Lord loves us all."

Does the Lord really love poor people? I asked myself. We were poor, without the provisions I thought we should have. I wanted to ask Sister Edwards why the Lord let my mother work so hard for so little. I didn't ask because to question the truth of her words would be disrespectful. So, I left my question alone and lived with my confusion.

Sister Edwards didn't need more problems. She often struggled to teach the lessons, not only because she was a stressed-out single mother of three but because she stuttered. I hoped she wouldn't try to pronounce any words that were longer than five letters, or we would be in for a long morning. All it took was one student to react rudely, and Sunday school would turn into hell.

For the life of me, I couldn't figure out why Pastor Jones didn't pick someone else to teach us. I'm not saying that Sister Edwards didn't do a good job. I'm just saying the pastor probably could have better used her services in an area that wouldn't have made her so vulnerable to ridicule. I saw frustration on many of the kids' faces and heard snickers from those less kind when she spoke. Kids interrupted Sister Edwards, then laughed when she tried to tell them not to be disrespectful. I don't know why she tried to pronounce *disrespectful* when she could have easily used any number of words with fewer syllables. I always felt somewhat bad for Sister Edwards because she had her own children in Sunday school, and they, too, were subjected to the mockery.

My brother James and I knew better than to make fun of Sister Edwards. If we had even thought about being rude to her, my mother would have beat our asses right there in front of the class and then made us stay there to endure the humiliation. Feeling helpless, I would sit back and watch the other children have their fun. I imagined a miracle happening and that their parents would come busting through the door and beat the shit

Syrup Sandwiches

out of them for being jerks. Maybe the other parents *did* teach respect as my mother did. Maybe they scolded their kids privately at home for teasing Sister Edwards. Whatever they might have done, it didn't make their kids any less rude.

One Sunday when I was ten, I remember James and me sitting on the floor in a group while Sister Edwards once again struggled to get out the word *disrespectful*. Finally, this time, she backed off and said, "bad mannered." But by that time the bedlam had been unleashed. Over the children's whoops and hollers, I couldn't hear the rest of what she said. James looked at me as if I could do something and I shrugged. There was a pitcher of grape Kool-Aid on the table behind me. I imagined pouring it all on Steve, the biggest loudmouth. But I didn't want to get myself in trouble.

Then James urged, "Say something."

I hesitated. The kids were quieting down anyway. But then they started up again with a roar of laughter. So, I stood and, with the loudest and most authoritative voice that I could muster, said, "Will you all stop talking!"

Sister Edwards fell silent. And to my surprise, so did the noisy children. They all looked at me. They were shocked—the quiet one had spoken. James held in his laughter, but I could see the smile on his face.

To my surprise, Sister Edwards said, "Thank you, Anthony." Then she continued to teach as if nothing had happened. But something had happened. The class was now respectful. And I felt some of that respect directed at me. The incident had a positive effect on me, showing me that I could make a difference by standing up for what was right.

Quiet kid that I was, there was another time that I shared the positive attention of the class with Sister Edwards. It was two years before, when I was eight and

James was six. Back then, like many little Sunday school boys, James and I wore clip-on ties. I wore a silver clip-on, and James wore a black one. They would often slip off at church, and they didn't seem like real men's ties to me. We did have two long, regular ties that sat in a drawer at home. What we didn't have was a man who could tie them for us and show us how to tie them ourselves.

So, one day I brought my untied blue tie to Sunday school, hoping I could find a man at church to teach me how to tie it. The classroom was in the basement area of the church, along with member meeting rooms. I looked in all the rooms down the hall to see if there was an older boy or man who might help me, but it was so early that there were only empty rooms filled with tables and chairs.

It was almost seven, so instead of going upstairs to find someone, I went to my Sunday school classroom, tie in hand. Before I could sit down on the hard floor, Sister Edwards startled me, "Anthony, what are you doing with that tie?"

I felt a little ashamed to be caught with an untied tie in my hand. It was like being told to tie your loose shoelaces when you are in first grade, and you don't know how to tie shoes yet. I hadn't planned to show Sister Edwards the tie. I'd assumed that, like my mother, she wouldn't know how to tie a man's tie.

"Good morning, Sister Edwards," was all I said, hoping she would forget her question to me.

But she persisted, "Anthony, do you need help with that tie?"

"Yes." I said, not meeting her eyes.

To my surprise, Sister Edwards showed me how to tie my tie. First, she tied it for me. Then she showed me a trick. Step by step she walked me through tying a knot in the tie on a desk and then putting the loose loop

Syrup Sandwiches

over my head before pulling it snug. Other children came into the classroom, and one boy asked what we were doing. So, Sister Edwards demonstrated how to tie a tie, step by step, in front of the whole class, using me as a model. Then she let me do it myself, following her instructions. I noticed some of the other boys in the class took a keen interest. They were the ones wearing clip-on ties. They probably also didn't have a man in the family who could teach them. But I showed them I could tie my own tie—even in front of the class. Sister Edwards assured them they could do it too.

It took a lot of practicing to get tie-tying down. Ultimately, I did, and I felt proud to be able to teach James how to tie a real tie. Later, when I taught my own son how to tie a tie using that special trick, I thought back to how Sister Edwards had taught me. In fact, to this day, I catch myself thinking of her guidance whenever I put on my tie and often smile. I find it intriguing how some scenes your mind won't forget.

Little by little, over the years, Sister Edwards did get through to me on other matters besides tie-tying. From her lessons I learned the value of forgiveness. I realized that I wasn't better than anyone, nor was anyone better than I. Eventually, I forgave the other kids for being thoughtless. I understood that Sister Edwards's stutter didn't make her less worthy. I began to see her as courageous. She could have easily given up teaching and served the church as an usher or a greeter. But she kept teaching because she did love each of us.

After Sunday school was over, the nine o'clock service began, which was the warmup for the bigger, traditional eleven o'clock morning service. Even for this early service there was a crowd waiting outside of the church to get in: men in dark suits and polished shoes, women in vibrant dresses with wide-brim hats. They all smiled and shook hands in greeting, exchanging friendly good mornings. I used to wonder how everyone could be so happy on Sunday. If I saw some of the same men and women on a Monday or Tuesday, they'd look worried and sad. The smiles on their faces had been replaced with stress. I could only imagine that the reality of it all was the fact that Sunday was a day of happiness, and the rest of the week was reality—back to the same difficult and challenging life that existed before.

When the Church doors opened, my brother and I were the first to follow the pastor and his entourage. We knew our mother would be looking for us, and we didn't want to worry her that we'd gotten lost on the way. Our mother or another uniformed usher would hand us a bulletin that listed the upcoming events, guest preachers, schedule, and people who were sick or shut in. After many years going to the church, I realized that the longer the bulletin, the longer the service.

These days our Baptist church in Brooklyn would be considered a *megachurch,* but back then, it was just a large church with a lot of people. The service at eleven was a big deal on Sundays. We had both an adult and a children's choir. Each choir marched down the aisles with pomp and circumstance while the musicians played, then they'd slowly transition toward the large choir seating area which was behind the pastor and announcer. After announcements, they sang a few more songs, followed by more announcements and prayer. I enjoyed listening to the choirs—to me, that was the best part of going to church. Then came tithe collections and love offerings, also called pastor's appreciation offerings. The finale was the building fund drive.

The church would frequently collect money. Pastor Jones was one of those preachers who told you like it was and wasn't afraid to piss off his congregation. He would often preach about people robbing God if they didn't pay their ten percent in tithes. He regularly said, "The Lord loves a cheerful giver."

Everyone in the church stood for the collections. The ushers, including my mother, directed each person to the closest aisle to proceed to the front, where the church deacons held round wicker contribution baskets. There was a time when the church would pass a collection plate from pew to pew, but I guess the plates were coming up short. Some congregants may have been taking instead of giving. So, to make sure that no one robbed God, the pastor watched people put their money into the basket from the pulpit.

After the collection was over, the choir sang another song, and then, finally, the pastor spoke. By this time, I was ready to go home. But the pastor could be counted on to preach a thought-provoking sermon with full conviction. He would preach and shout and preach some more. His slated forty-five-minute sermon often lasted an hour and a half.

I loved to people watch during his long sermons to see who would be the first to nod off. As soon as I saw a sleeper, I'd brace myself for the inevitable—the pastor would holler into the microphone, "Can I get an Amen?"

Sometimes it was difficult not to nod off myself, but I knew that if my mother caught me sleeping, I would never hear the end of it. Staying awake in church, I did learn a few things from our preacher. There were two messages he had incorporated into many sermons that I have never forgotten. First, "Never be afraid to say what's on your mind if you do it in a respectful manner." And second, "You can't win every battle, so knowing when to fight is just as important as winning."

When the pastor was finally done preaching, he asked the congregation, "Is there anyone in the audience who wants to be saved? If so, please come down to the altar." As the choir sang softly to the slow-tempo music, we would sit, waiting for people to get out of their seats and head to the altar. Sometimes there were a few people who went to the altar, and other times there were no takers. After that long process was over, the pastor would ask, "Is there anyone who wants to join the church? Please come to the altar."

Between the pastor holding out for people to either turn their lives over to God or for new guests to join the church, I see why we never could get out of the eleven o'clock service which often lasted until two or three in the afternoon. The church also sold dinners on Sunday; so, when we could afford it, which was rare, we would stay and eat at the church. Usually, we would leave the service with only enough time to go home and have a dinner that had been prepared the night before. Then it was time to go back to church for the evening service that started at five o'clock. The evening service would go on and on until the preacher couldn't stand up anymore. That meant we didn't see home again until it was nighttime. James and I would get a sense of hope when we'd see the preacher sit down. That's when we knew that he was getting tired and that the service would be ending soon.

Without question, the woman-led Owens family would be at all services. Sundays were the Lord's Day, and Rena Owens made sure we belonged to the Lord on that day. Yes, we were deprived of much, but my mother believed that God was the answer. She would go to church, hear the sermon, and pray.

Sometimes, I would wonder how enormous our church would be if as many men joined as women. Our church had far more women than men. And when I asked my mother about it, she said, "Men like sports more."

I thought that was an odd response, but I could understand how sports could be more fun than going to church and giving up money. Most black men were probably too busy trying to make a living, whether for themselves or their families. I could imagine that most of them didn't want to give up their hard-earned money to the church. Besides, the women in their families were probably like my mother and already diverting money needed for household expenses to the church.

Most of the men who attended my church were either deacons or sang in the choir. I saw men scattered throughout the congregation but nothing close to the number of women and children. The women of the church were the foundation, and they made sure that things ran efficiently. In my eyes, they kept the church going, and without them the church would have closed.

It was strange that I never heard the pastor encourage men to join the church or address the importance of men being there for their children. I was never provided the opportunity to build a relationship with any of the men in church. When I became a teenager, I started to notice that many of the men in church seemed more interested in the women who came to church in their tight dresses than talking to me or my brother. I noticed deacons openly staring at women's asses as they walked down the aisles to drop their money into the collection baskets. I guess mentoring fatherless boys was far from their minds.

Ordinarily, my mother brought us to church on Wednesday nights for Bible study and then on Sundays for Sunday school, the early morning service, the conventional service, and the evening service. But when there was a revival, we would go to church every single day for a whole week. Sometimes these revivals would be held in tents on vacant lots around the neighborhood like southern revivals you see in old movies. Our high-energy Brooklyn church revivals galvanized all the members to bring their neighbors to church and enticed passersby. A line-up of powerful guest preachers leading a series of jam-packed services got sinners to repent and join our church. Thankfully, Brooklyn revivals were usually only held once a year. Church was exciting to adults during revival week, but as an elementary school-aged child, the last thing that I wanted to do was sit in a pew with my mother every night of the week in a church filled with mostly grown-ups. Heck, watching the same J trains come and go from the fire escape while James and I talked seemed like more fun. I couldn't understand why parents would bring their young children to a church filled predominately with adults to listen to an adult preach about things that most children didn't understand. Did the parents expect for the child to be saved, anointed, and become as devoted as they were just because they sat in a pew every day of the revival?

I said to my mother, "Rena, why do me and James have to go to revival all week?"

Her response was as expected, "Y'all lucky to be able to see so many people being saved and to hear all these great preachers. In Georgia, I went to church for revival every day for two weeks instead of one." Then whispering, as if she didn't want nearby church members to feel too terribly disadvantaged, "And our revival was not once but twice a year."

Churchgoing was central to my childhood. There were times, however, when my mother didn't take us to church. That was when she didn't have any money for the collection basket. When my mother did have money to give, it was usually her last bit of cash. As I grew, I resented it more and more that she gave money that we needed to the church. But she gave because the preacher said, "The Lord will make a way out of no way," and she really believed that.

Syrup Sandwiches

Although my mother prayed to God for help, I only remember her asking the church for help one time. After over a decade as a member of the church, she didn't feel it was unreasonable to go to the church for a one-time financial assistance request. I was fourteen at the time, and we had been living for years in our own apartment in Bushwick. My mother was behind on the rent and afraid we'd be evicted from of our apartment. She contacted the church treasurer for an appointment, who set up a time to meet her at our apartment.

I was the one who answered our door when the treasurer knocked. I knew the tall, skinny, steel-haired lady at the door because I would see her almost every Sunday.

She said, "Hello, young man, is your mother here?"

"Yes, in the other room," I said.

Mother was happily surprised that the treasurer had come to the apartment before their set appointment. They hugged and then I knew to go into the other room. My mother frequently told James and me, "Never get into grown-folk business." When adults were talking, we knew not to interrupt. But from the other room I could hear them. The conversation started with the good news about some church member who had recovered from an illness. Then the treasurer lowered her voice and turned businesslike.

"The church can't afford to help people out with their rent; if we do it for you, then we would have to do it for everyone," she said.

There was a moment of silence. I held myself back from running into the room. Then my mother said, "Are you telling me that the church can't help me this one time—and I've been giving money to this church for ten years! I have never even once asked the church for anything."

The Treasurer said, "I'm sorry, Sister Owens." Without waiting for my mother to stand up, she walked out.

My mother was angry and hurt. So was I. My mother would give her last dime to the church. The last thing that she wanted to do was "rob God." But she was disappointed that her church wouldn't work with God to "make a way out of no way" to help her. My mother was confused. And when she was confused, she prayed. I was too angry to pray.

Year after year, as a child, I prayed with my mother at home and at church. We prayed for safety, wealth, and good health. Growing up black and seeing how much everyone that I knew struggled, especially in the South, I prayed for strength not to let the struggles that life has and will inflict upon me ruin me as a person. I prayed for the ability to do better to provide for the family I wanted to have than my family was able to do for me. Often it seemed as if the more we prayed, the more difficult things became. Many times, my prayers—like my mother's—weren't answered. However, for us, turning our backs on God or even the church that would not help us pay one month's rent was not an option. When you're raised in a church, that's all you know. You grow up without any doubt that this church is where your belief and faith belong. We had the church and prayers while we were struggling, hungry, afraid, and confused. There was nothing else.

I know that it might be hard to understand why so many black people in America still remain steadfast churchgoers with unshakable faith in God. I have grappled with this myself. Often, as a child and into my adulthood, I would see racial inequality and think, *why do black people have to go through so much?* I'd question if there was a God. I started believing that God didn't like black people. I couldn't understand how black American people could be discriminated against and treated so unfairly yet stay in church praying. I started to pray for equality, just as many other blacks before me have done. Would my prayers go unanswered, just like theirs? I knew that as black Americans we had to prove ourselves over and over. Things were even worse when I was a child in this regard. When we'd do everything that we thought we needed to do to shore up our side of the playing field, we'd still lose out. Yet, as a community our faith remained strong.

Time and again, I witnessed that working hard and becoming educated and articulate was not enough. When there are no answers, prayer becomes more enticing. Consider this: Who doesn't turn to prayer in a time of crisis or when facing an impossible task? Even an atheist might pray when a tornado heads toward them. So, it's no wonder that black Americans regularly turn to prayer. I believe that if it wasn't for praying and having something to believe in, my journey to this point would have been much more difficult. Although many of my prayers haven't been answered, I'd rather keep believing that one day they will be than to give up and lose all hope.

If I had not adopted my church's teachings on prayer and faith as a child with the common ritual of joining a community of passionate people endeavoring to endure, there is no telling who I would have become. Would I be as caring, thoughtful, or considerate? Would I even be alive? I know I make church sound like it was a long, drawn-out bore for me as a child. In some ways it was, but I loved going anyway. Church was my escape from depression and loneliness. It was a safe place that helped me stay grounded. Living in a confusing world, I liked being part of something that I felt was positive and productive.

Many of the children in the church didn't have both a mother and a father in their lives. Like James and me, they appeared normal on the surface. Sure, they were probably as poor as we were, but when you're used to struggling and going without, you learn how to mask your emotions, hunger, and loneliness. We never spoke about not having a father in the house. The few children I knew who had fathers were like the rest of us but with one exception—they seemed happier.

I remember my mother and the pastor telling me many times that to get to heaven I must turn my life over to Christ. I learned at a young age that this turning over my life involved three steps: I must confess my sins, acknowledge Christ as my personal Savior, and I had to be baptized. Momentous, life-changing steps. I had watched many people go through the process, and so could I, I thought.

By the time I was fifteen, I'd completed two of the three steps. The baptism would complete the trifecta. You might think the first two requirements would have been the hardest but not for me. I was nervous about being submerged under the water. I was afraid that I might drown. I was a teenager yet didn't know how to swim.

Before his Sunday sermon, the pastor asked everyone who was planning to get baptized that day to meet in the back of the church. There were about fifteen of us. We were all handed robes to wear and sent to dressing rooms to change for the ritual. When the sermon was completed, the pastor led the rest of the congregation to another area of the church where there was a large aboveground swimming pool and seating for spectators. My mother, brother, and sister sat there wide-eyed, filled with anticipation as the pastor baptized person after person. When it was my turn, I walked up the four rungs of the ladder leading to the pool where the pastor stood waist-deep in the water. As I stepped into the cold water, my immediate thought was to turn around and leave. But I couldn't embarrass and disappoint my family and myself, so I moved through the water toward the pastor. To prepare, the pastor asked me to fold my hands across my chest.

Then he said, "Today we acknowledge your old self is buried with Christ and you have been raised to new life in Jesus. Therefore, Anthony, I now baptize you in the name of the Father, the Son, and of the Holy Spirit."

He told me to hold my nose, and then he put one hand behind me and the other in front. Into the water he submerged me. Then immediately he pulled me up. I was now baptized. My vision blurred from the pool water, I recognized my mother's voice yell out, "Amen." When my eyes cleared, I saw her crying for joy.

My brother James and my sister Rhonda sat there in silent amazement, almost motionless. I can still see the look of awe on their faces. As I stood there nervous, soaking wet, and cold, I was waiting with anticipation for awe to hit me. I expected to feel a moment of epiphany, an awakening, something. However, nothing happened. What's the purpose of baptism, I wondered, if it didn't make you feel anything? Was a baptism just something to say that you've done, like a check in the box? Maybe I was too young to know the magnitude or importance of being baptized. However, to say that I was disappointed would have been an understatement.

Chapter 3
Grandparents

We were regular churchgoers in Brooklyn because my mother had gone to church with her mother and siblings as a child in Georgia. Church was where they felt safe and happy, she told me.

Their shotgun home in the small, Peanut Belt town of Dawson wasn't a safe and happy place. My mother told me that, as a child, she sometimes picked cotton and packed it into large sacks, but mostly she worked on a peanut farm. She remembered that, as a girl, she couldn't get the smell of peanuts out of her clothes or off her mind. But what my mother never got over, even after she moved, were the stories that her mother, Linda, would tell her about Oscar, my mother's father. My grandfather hadn't only neglected my grandmother and their children, but he would also emotionally and physically abuse her. Whenever Rena would talk to me about my grandmother's life, she would do so in between tears. I felt bad for asking about my grandmother; but knowing so little about her, I wanted to learn all that I could. What I came to understand from what my mother did share was that my grandfather often yelled at my grandmother and slapped her anytime he didn't like what she said.

With a man she couldn't trust to take care of them, it was no wonder her mother looked heavenward for love and support and made the church her refuge.

"God should be the most important person in your life," my grandmother told my mother when she was a little girl.

My grandfather, Oscar, was what you would call a *broke hustler*. He would do anything to make a buck. He sold everything from cookies to clothing but mostly pipe dreams. He did any odd job to make money because he didn't have a real trade. His hustling and bartering never paid off until later in life when he was finally successful enough to purchase a laundromat in New York City.

My grandmother, Linda, was my grandfather's common-law wife and a homemaker who depended on him for all her financial needs. My grandmother was a passive, soft-spoken woman who was accommodating and kindhearted. She would give anything to anyone. She loved to smile and enjoyed making others smile. My mother told me that her mother would open her home to other families in the neighborhood who had even less than she had. She would invite them over to dinner and sometimes allowed them to stay overnight when they had no other place to go.

Unfortunately, she would often cower in fear from Oscar, who would drink alcohol for no other reason than it was available to him. Time and time again my grandfather would come home smelling of both alcohol and perfume. Then he would begin to argue with my grandmother about anything to avoid her asking about his obvious escapades.

There were times when my grandfather would be gone for three days, only to return and claim that he had been out of town working. Then, in a humble tone and a pleasant voice, he would ask my grandmother, "What's for dinner?"

My mother believed that her father only returned because he knew that he could get away with treating her mother cruelly. She knew it wasn't my grandmother's great cooking or the children that they had together that kept him coming back, it was her vulnerability. My mother said, "If my mother had put her foot down, even once, maybe my father would have changed." At least that's what she thought.

My grandmother knew that my grandfather was cheating on her. Even though they were never legally married, she treated him like a husband. Even though she had given birth to his five children, he treated her like just another girlfriend.

My grandmother told my mother that in the 1940s and 1950s most of the black families that they knew were primarily concerned with survival. They weren't so much concerned about a formal marriage as they were about feeding their families and not being killed by white people who were racist. She would tell me, "Back then, black people problems weren't the same as white people problems."

My mother said that my grandmother wanted to marry Oscar, but my grandfather mulishly refused. My grandmother could not control her phony husband and his desire for other women nor could she stop his unfaithful behavior no matter how hard she tried.

My mother believed that my grandfather took advantage of her mother because she never spoke up for herself and allowed him to go unchecked. Apparently, Oscar wasn't the only one who took advantage of her patience and generosity. Even as a young child, my mother would tell her mother to stop being so freehearted to everyone. But Oscar was relentless. His abuse went on for years. My grandmother's strongest tactic was to prepare fried chicken, collards, macaroni and cheese, and

Syrup Sandwiches

cornbread—my grandfather's favorite meal—to keep him in the house. It never worked. He saw her passivity and kindness as a weakness to exploit. He could live untethered yet have a dependable woman to come home to and mistreat.

My mother shared that my grandmother would ask God to stop my grandfather from cheating and hurting her. My grandmother had such hope that deep down he was a good man. She explained to my mother that Oscar was the sweetest and kindest man that she had ever met but after she started having his children, he changed. "It was like he didn't have eyes for me anymore."

My mother told me that when her father was gone for a long time, her mother would sit at home and cry. My mother could never understand how her mother continued to love a man who would beat her, cheat on her, and leave her all alone with their children.

After my grandfather had been unfaithful and disrespectful to her for years, my grandmother told him he needed to leave those other women alone or she would leave him. She meant it. His actions had become so destructive that she couldn't take it anymore. But before she figured out how to leave the man whom she once loved, he left her.

My grandfather moved to Brooklyn, New York, in 1946. To pursue bigger dreams, he left behind the devoted and loving mother of his four young children while she was carrying his fifth child. My mother was two at the time; her oldest sibling, only nine. They would grow up without their father in the house. Thankfully, they had the assistance of my grandmother's sisters and brother to help them scrape by financially.

A few years after my grandfather left, my grandmother found comfort in another man, Nelson

Cole. Nelson was a gentle man, all of six feet tall, with an almost perfect smile, and the charm to go along with it. My mother once told me that he would brush his jet black and wavy hair until the sun's reflection could be seen in his radiant mane. My grandmother loved Nelson, not for just being the man that she desired and deserved but for his thoughtfulness and the love that he showed her in return. He was soft spoken and knew how to comfort my grandmother when she felt irritable during stressful times. Nelson didn't drink or smoke and treated my grandmother and her children like they were his family. He was in love with Linda, and he showed her respect. My mother told me that her mother was the happiest that she had ever seen, and it made her feel good that her mother had finally found someone who truly loved her.

My grandmother and Nelson had a daughter together and named her Lillie. They had a son named Justin, two years later. This gave my grandmother a total of seven children. This number wasn't unusual. In those days, it was common to have larger families with many children. My grandmother worked part-time as a home attendant for a white family, and Nelson worked at the peanut farm. My mother's older brother and sister also worked at the peanut farm. They could only work part-time at first because they were still children. The four salaries barely provided for the family, but they made do with what they had.

My mother told me that Nelson had proposed to my grandmother. Two years after the birth of Justin, they were about to get married when Nelson was killed in a car accident. He was walking home from work one evening when he was hit by a car. The driver drover off and never even stopped to help Nelson. The hit-and-run driver was never found. Nelson died at the scene of the accident, his body so mangled and ripped apart that he

Syrup Sandwiches

had to have a closed-casket funeral. My mother told me that her mother was devastated and inconsolable. She had no one there who could hold her as she wept night after night. It was almost as if the life had been sucked completely out of her. She didn't smile anymore, and the things that she once loved, like crocheting and reading, were replaced with tears and silence.

A few years later, my aunts, Odessa and Denise, and my uncles, Fred and Daniel, moved to New York and lived together in an apartment in the Fort Greene section of Brooklyn. My Aunt Odessa died six years later. When the news got back to my grandmother and the rest of the family back in Georgia, they were in shock. My grandmother took the news extremely hard, especially because my aunt had died from kidney failure. Her death seemed as if it could have been prevented. My mother told me that Odessa didn't like to drink water, and no one could make her drink it. My mother told me that she was so heartbroken when Odessa died and how she remembered Odessa braiding her hair and helping her with her homework.

"Anthony, I couldn't believe that my sister was dead," she confided to me. "It took me a long time to be OK."

Full of grief, my grandmother blamed Oscar, for not looking after Odessa, their first-born daughter, while she was living in Brooklyn. Odessa didn't live with my grandfather. He'd had nothing to do with her the whole time she lived in Brooklyn. So, if lack of caring had contributed to her death, then he was certainly guilty. My grandfather did attend the funeral, along with my uncles, Fred and Daniel, and my aunt Denise. My grandmother was the only one from Georgia to attend. My mother and Aunt Lillie were both pregnant, and Justin stayed behind with them. My grandmother took the long bus ride to

New York all alone. I can only imagine that she had a lot of time to cry, think, and pray during her ride.

    In Brooklyn, Grandfather Oscar, started another family. He decided to marry his new love interest, Susan, or Little-Bit, as we called her, two years after he buried his oldest daughter. I wondered how he could have five children by my grandmother and never marry her and then turn around and marry a lady that he hardly knew.

    I was eight when I first met my grandfather's wife, Little-Bit. My mother had taken James and me on a rare visit to our grandfather so that she could ask him for some money for groceries. I'll never forget how this tiny woman looked at me. It was as if she didn't see James or my mother. She was an adult at my eye level, and she stared at me for about a minute before looking away. I had been stared at before by others, but the stare that she gave me sent chills down my spine. She scrunched up her face as if she smelled a terrible odor and was going to dispose of me like a dead Brooklyn rat. I immediately looked away.

    At first, I figured I'd done something rude. But I hadn't said anything other than hello. I checked my shoes to see if I'd tracked anything in. As I looked back up, she was still staring. She stopped the frightening glare only after my grandfather entered the room and spoke to us.

    I asked my mother when we left their apartment if she'd noticed the stare. "Anthony, she does that to everyone," she said.

    When I grew old enough to consider genetics, I started to wonder if she'd reacted fiercely to me because I looked too much like her husband. There was no doubt that I was his grandson. As his grandson, I was proof of his children from a previous relationship that she didn't want to see. She openly hated that her husband had fathered children with another woman. My mother told me that she overheard Little-Bit tell my grandfather, "Don't spend any of our money on your ex or her children." She said "her" children, as if they were not her husband's children too.

My mother told me that my grandfather had the reputation as a ladies' man even when my grandmother had met him. But he'd charmed her into thinking that he'd change once they became a couple. He was six foot four and handsome, weighing about 165 pounds fully dressed and soaking wet with bricks in his pockets. He had what some would call "good hair," the kind that looked like it was freshly permed. I believe that my mother inherited her good hair from him.

I knew from family stories that my grandfather could have his choice in women. So, I could never figure out what he saw in Little-Bit. Her hair wouldn't grow longer than a half inch. She was only five feet tall, wearing heels, yet her shoes were size eleven. Oscar would sometimes slip her shoes on by mistake in the dark. Her hands were small like her body, and one of her palms had hair on it. She wasn't even a nice person.

My mother never believed in voodoo, but she said that Little-Bit had a magic spell on my grandfather. After my grandmother had tried and failed for years to rein in my grandfather, his cheating days were officially over when he met Little-Bit. Little-Bit wouldn't have any of that nonsense, and under her spell, he forgot about anybody and everybody else.

We noticed that she was terribly sweet to my grandfather, and that probably explained why he loved her so blindly. It didn't even seem to matter one bit that she openly disdained his children and grandchildren. Although my grandfather could sometimes get his way with his smile and smooth talk, I remember that underneath he appeared confused and vacant and would often distance himself from my mother, as if trying not to interact with both his wife and his daughter at the same time. With Little-Bit, his puppeteer, he was manipulated to make even more selfish decisions. Afraid to annoy her, he often forgot the children who still needed him. He never welcomed our visits to him, especially with his wife guarding the door. But when I was thirteen, I learned to manipulate him a little bit myself.

My mother had sent James and me to ask my grandfather for money. She told us that Little-Bit went to the grocery in the middle of the afternoon. So, we watched from a shadowy doorway across the street until Little-Bit left before we entered his apartment building. Our grandfather greeted us at the door with a Camel cigarette in his hand and abruptly said, "Are you boys here because your mother sent you?"

I knew that if I said yes, he would be upset and wouldn't give my mother the few dollars she needed. I casually said, "No, we were out walking near your neighborhood and decided to stop by."

Squinting and cocking his head, he bent down to look me in the eyes. He didn't believe a word that I'd said. He then blew the thick Camel smoke at our faces. Undeterred, as the cloud of smoke dissipated, we walked into the apartment. The apartment could have looked better. It had two bedrooms, a kitchen, a living room, and a bathroom. But the furniture was old, and the terrible smell smoke had soaked into the upholstery and drapes. Even the plants seemed to be dying.

I'd never had any real conversations with my grandfather. I'd once overheard him say, "I don't like talking to children," and he behaved as if that were true. But without Little-Bit there, I felt I could try striking up a conversation.

I started with small talk, telling him about our grades and what schools we were in and then mentioned

Syrup Sandwiches

how hot it was outside. To my surprise, my grandfather asked us, "What do you want to be when you grow up?"

I told him I didn't know what I wanted to be when I grew up, but I liked English best at school. James said he liked math and wanted to do something with that.

"You boys don't know how good you have it to be living in Brooklyn. The South was hell. They used to chase us all the way home from school." He looked at us with a wide-eyed intensity that rattled us.

"Who was *they*?" I asked. I was imagining a pack of wolves.

He hesitated, then angrily said, "Those white boys. Life was terrible in Georgia. That's why I moved to Brooklyn."

I didn't know what to say. But for the first time I felt a connection with my grandfather. I had only known about the bad things he'd done. I hadn't considered that bad things had been done to him. Thinking back, I realize that he, like the rest of my family, had probably gone through many traumatic experiences—experiences that had affected him in ways that I will never be able to fully understand.

After some silence, I changed the subject. "My mother mentioned that if we stopped by to see you, to ask if you could send her a few dollars to help get some groceries." My grandfather put his hand into his pocket and pulled out a wad of cash, looked me in my eyes, and said, "Here's ten dollars. Now you boys go home."

I remember a year or so later going alone to my grandfather's apartment when he was playing cards with some of his friends. Again, I was there to get some money for my mother. As I walked into his smoke-filled apartment, one of the card players said, "Oscar, is that your grandson?"

My grandfather said nonchalantly, "That's one of them."

The way that he said it made me wish I hadn't been there. Then the same card player exclaimed, "Wow, he's tall like you."

My grandfather gave him a half smile and asked what I wanted.

"My mother asked if you had a few dollars for some groceries." I spoke up and addressed the whole table of card players. I figured he wouldn't want to look cheap or broke in front of them.

After getting twelve dollars and leaving, I played back in my mind that card player comparing me to my grandfather, and it instantly angered me. I never wanted to be compared to Oscar in any way. That man wasn't like me. I was certainly not like him. Sure, he'd had it rough as a kid. However, I thought that if he'd done the right thing as a father, my mother's childhood probably wouldn't have been so rough. My life wouldn't have been so rough. At fourteen, I had already decided that I wouldn't allow myself to grow up like him. There was no way that I could see myself abandoning my children.

Chapter 4
Time for a Change

My grandmother, Linda, at age forty-seven, decided that it was time to move from Georgia to Brooklyn to escape the Jim Crow South. She hoped that the North would be more accepting of her race and could provide some relief and opportunities that weren't available for her and her children where she came from. She also wanted to leave behind a place that held the memory of Nelson's horrible accident, the death of her daughter, and her crushed heart. My mother, Aunt Lillie, Uncle Justin, my cousins (Annette and Julie), James, and I all headed to New York with my grandmother. James and Annette were infants. My cousin Julie and I were two. My mother was twenty-one, Aunt Lillie, seventeen, and Uncle Justin, fifteen.

My Aunt Lillie had her first child at fifteen and the second not long before we left. My mother had given birth to me at age nineteen, the same age that her mother gave birth to her first child. For most of my life, all I knew about my birth was the date. But fifty-eight years after I was born, my mother stunned me with the story of my delivery. "I was at home alone in Georgia when you were born, and there was no one there to help me," she said. "My brother and sister were in school, and my mother was at work. I didn't know what to do, so I grabbed a bunch of towels and laid in the bed confused and in pain. I screamed and screamed but no one heard me. Then out you came."

I was at a loss for words. I could not imagine how difficult and scary that must have been. All I could say was, "Thank you, I love you."

After she gave birth to me, her mother came home, saw the blood, and exclaimed in a panic, "What have you done, what have you done!"

Fortunately, my clearheaded Aunt Lillie came in a few minutes later, saw what had happened, then she immediately ran out of the house to locate a midwife. When the midwife came, she tended to my mother and cut the umbilical cord.

My brother James was born two years after me. We have different fathers, but coincidentally, we both have the same birthdate, only two years apart. Go figure. My brother and I wondered for years how that could have happened. We think that our fathers came to see our mother around Christmas time, bearing gifts and smiles, and then next thing you know, guess who's pregnant! We might be wrong, but it sure is a damn good guess.

When my mother decided to leave with her mother for New York, she did not tell my father or James's father that she was moving away. She just left and didn't look back. That move would ultimately have consequences—not so much for my mother but for her children. She would learn that two boys needed their fathers more than she'd thought they would. But back then, leaving Georgia was in many ways a sensible decision. My mother, Rena, did not want to raise a newborn and a two-year-old as a single parent without support from her mother or siblings in the racist South. She, too, was hoping that New York, surrounded by family, would give her a better chance at a new life. Life was so difficult that it was hard to imagine it not being better. And I suspect that by the time my mother moved from Georgia, she had become so accustomed to not having her father around, she felt that James and I didn't need a father around either.

I remember once saying to my mother, "Rena, do you know how we can get in touch with our fathers?" At first, she appeared to not have heard me, then I repeated my question. She replied matter-of-factly, "I don't know how to find them," with a look on her face as if my question annoyed her.

For James and me, it was difficult not knowing who our fathers were, where they were, or what they looked like. My father would be absent through my entire childhood and adolescent years, and James would never find his father. Our mother would never try to contact them to let them know where we were. When I became old enough to understand the enormity of her decision to cut us off from our fathers, I wanted to be angry with my mother. But I knew that as a young parent, trying to get her footing, and trying to provide for James and me, she didn't need me to pile on pointless grief about our fathers.

Fleeing Georgia and our fathers had taken guts, but my mother did it bolstered with the courage and hope of her mother and support from her siblings. Only two at the time, I can only imagine what the trip must have been like for our family, crammed into that northbound Greyhound bus. My grandmother was familiar with the long ride to New York, since she had just taken it two years earlier to bury her oldest daughter, but the rest of us had never been out of Georgia. My mother's older brother and sister had moved to New York at least five years prior and were living together. So, when we arrived in Brooklyn, we all stayed in the three-story brownstone that my uncle and aunt were renting.

Life in Brooklyn didn't turn out quite like my mother expected. She was twenty-one with two children, unemployed, and not educated enough or street savvy enough to cope with the big-city life. She had to learn how to deal with the hustle and bustle of a fast-paced city that was now unfamiliar turf. Neither my father nor James's father was there to provide any sort of financial or emotional support. My mother never said that she regretted not telling our fathers where we were and went on with life as if it wasn't an issue. Maybe she thought they would not have provided any support even if they knew.

My mother didn't have any marketable skills and found it difficult to find stable employment, but she worked odd jobs, cleaning and caring for the elderly. She never gave up, no matter how many long hours she worked or how difficult and demanding the jobs were. There would be times when she would come home smelling like urine and feces. When I was seven, it was difficult to understand why my mother worked so hard. Looking back, I can see how my mother's relentless desire to provide for her children instilled in me a drive to be the best parent that I can be.

I would often ask her if there was anything that I could do to help, but she would usually say, "I'm OK, thanks." I knew that she was not OK because many nights I could hear her in the next room sobbing after she came home. Crying seemed to just make her more determined to do her best. In the early 70s my mother was making the minimum wage of $1.60 per hour, $64 a week before taxes. Even back then, her pay wasn't adequate. It certainly wasn't enough to support a family of three. With her meager salary and three mouths to feed, along with paying rent of $15 a week toward her brother and sister's apartment, she didn't have enough money to live on.

After working for nine years taking care of the elderly, my mother injured her back at work one night.

Syrup Sandwiches

She didn't qualify for disability at the time. Because she couldn't work, we had no income. So, my mother applied for welfare.

When my mother came home, I remember her telling me and James about the long lines at the welfare office that she had to wait in before she was called to the window. She looked so sad, I asked, "What's wrong?" She said to me, "Anthony, I never thought that I would be on welfare. I never wanted that."

I wasn't mature enough to realize that my mother was between a rock and a hard place, and she didn't like it. All I could say was, "It will be OK."

Eventually, my mother was able to get her own place in a section of Brooklyn called Bushwick, and I will never forget that apartment. We lived on the fourth floor, which was the top floor of an all-brick, eight-family apartment building. Most apartment buildings in Brooklyn and throughout New York's five boroughs had fire escapes that were either in the front or back of the building. Our fire escape was in the front of the building which gave James and me front row balcony seats to the sounds and sights of our neighborhood.

Sometimes I would go with my mother when she had enough money to go grocery shopping at the A&P, which was four blocks from our apartment on Broadway Avenue. A&P was short for The Great Atlantic & Pacific Tea Company, and it was founded in New York City in 1859. During the 1970s, A&P was the largest grocery store chain in the United States. I would see young boys around my age packing grocery bags and then escorting the customers out with their shopping carts. I thought to myself, *I could do that; it doesn't look that hard.*

On one occasion, after my mother was done shopping, we went home and unpacked the few groceries. Then I went back to A&P, and as I approached the store, I saw one of the baggers from earlier. This kid looked to be about my age. So, I walked up to him, no pleasantries spoken, and said, "Hey man, how did you get a job bagging? Are you really old enough?"

"I'm nine," he said. "The store don't mind who bags groceries, just as long as they don't have to pay us."

"Do you think I can get a job? I'm only eight," I said.

"I was eight when I started. It won't matter. Just show up for work."

"Thanks," I replied. "I'll see you tomorrow."

I was stoked and couldn't wait to go to work. The entire night I thought about working at A&P. The next day would be Saturday, and I knew the grocery store would be busy.

I was at the store as soon as they opened at eight in the morning. The first person that I saw was the kid that I met the day before. In my rudeness and hurry the day before, I'd forgotten to ask him his name.

"I'm Anthony. What's your name?" I asked.

"Jeff," he said and gave me a smile.

After the store opened, Jeff and I, along with about six other baggers, were up front waiting for customers to come through the door. By noon, we were all busy bagging. It was fun, and some customers would tip fifty cents or a dollar. Eventually, it added up. By Sunday, I had made fifteen dollars and was elated. I remember how proud my mother and James were of me for bagging groceries regularly and bringing home income.

The job could be entertaining as well. I remember one Saturday, another hot and blistering summer day in July. I had been working at A&P almost a year, and bagging was going great. It was around nine in the morning when a man walked into the store and started shopping, just like the other customers, but this man

Syrup Sandwiches

appeared to be talking to himself. I don't think anyone paid any attention to him, but I kept staring at him as he went from aisle to aisle. I thought he seemed strange. When he was done shopping and his grocery cart was full, this man calmly walked out of the store. The makeshift security guard tried to stop him, but the man violently pushed the guard to the floor, and the guard's head hit the porcelain tile and began to bleed. The robber rushed out with the grocery cart and quickly put the groceries into a waiting vehicle. Then he and the driver sped off. I was now nine years old, but I was still shocked to see something like that unfold before my eyes.

I questioned Jeff. "Had anyone ever done anything like that before?"

"Only a few times," he replied. "They normally just shoplift."

I thought that a person must really be desperate to have to steal food. Then I thought that maybe this man had a family at home that he couldn't provide for, and he had no other choice but to steal. Maybe he had children who were hungry like James and I were sometimes. So many scenarios came crashing through my mind. The police and paramedics came rushing into the store to help the battered security guard. I went home later, around, seven and told my mother and James what happened at work, and they were both stunned and felt bad for the guard.

As a child, I probably should have had more time playing with friends than working and trying to help my mother buy groceries. I would work a lot of hours at A&P trying to make as much money as possible to help my mother. I knew that between working and going to school and church that I wouldn't have a lot of time to play with friends. At first it bothered me that I wasn't having as much fun as some of the other children my age, but as I started to make money, even if it was a small amount, playing didn't matter as much. Looking back now, I can see how it might have been unfair for me to be working so young instead of enjoying my childhood but working at a young age taught me responsibility and the value of a dollar.

I was happy to have my brother for company when I came home from work. My brother and I would often sit on the fire escape and talk about anything and everything while we watched the people and the traffic below. We would sit out on the fire escape for hours. We'd talk about my working at the grocery store. I would explain to James how many bags of groceries I packed that day, the best way to pack bags, and which items should go in first. I'd say, "You should always try to pack the canned food and boxes first, that way you'll be able to fit more into the bag."
James was looking forward to being able to start working and would often say, "Man, you are lucky to be older."

Fire escapes are used for just that—to allow tenants to be able to escape their apartments in the event of an emergency, usually fires. It also provided a means for rescue officials to gain access to the victims who were trapped inside. The fire escape was a reprieve for James and me. Some of the things James and I saw from that fire escape were unimaginable and unbelievable. We lived on Broadway Avenue in the Northern part of Bushwick. We had a parallel view of the J trains and were in between the train stops of Gates Avenue and Halsey Street. The J train had tracks for the northbound and southbound lines and an express line that started between Myrtle and Marcy Avenues.
We could see the passengers on the trains, the trains filled with so many people that it looked like they

Syrup Sandwiches

were melted together as they sped by. At night, when the trains were not as crowded, we could see people eating, arguing, or even making out. What a view! The trains continually shook our building, day and night. I thought that I would get used to it, but I never really did. I finally found a place in my mind where I emotionally blocked out the noise, or so I thought. It only worked sometimes. Many nights I would be awakened out of my sleep because the last train passing seemed louder than the previous thirty-five that had passed earlier. *How is that possible?* I thought.

Below the train tracks was a terrific view of the streets and the vehicles that often jammed them, not to mention the herd of people that seemed to be on the same mission of making as much noise as humanly possible. There were many traffic jams on Broadway, normally caused by city buses that stopped at almost every other block to pick up and drop off people. Sitting on the fire escape, James and I could smell the exhaust fumes from the influx of vehicles.

The apartment had two bedrooms, a living room, kitchen, and bathroom. When we moved in, it looked spacious to me, but then again, I was only eight years old. At that age, a bathroom would have seemed large to me. We did have more room than we had at my aunt and uncle's brownstone. This would be home for many years as James and I grew up.

Chapter 5
Greg

With everything that my mother had going on in her life—being broke as hell, giving money she didn't have to the church, and trying to feed two growing boys and herself—she still couldn't escape her sexual desires and need for companionship. In retrospect, I know now that she needed and wanted someone to hold her at night, make love to her, and tell her that everything would be all right. My mother met a man named Greg while going to church one Sunday morning. James and I saw him talking to her while in church but didn't think anything about it. I assumed they were having the same boring conversations adults usually have at church, or so we thought. Three days later, we see this same man at our apartment. I thought that he was there to maybe talk more about church stuff with my mother. Boy was I wrong!

My mother introduced him to us, and he proudly said, "Hey, boys, my name is Greg. I'm your mother's friend." He said it with a smirk on his face and smiled as if he knew something that we didn't know.

My mother loved to smile, showing her large, gapped top teeth. I thought that gapped teeth looked better on females than it did on men. I inherited the same large gap that my mother had, and I hated it. But her teeth made her distinctively appealing. My mother also stood out because she was five foot ten and a vigorous 165 pounds. So, my attractive, tall mother meets this stout, short man. He was probably five four if he stood on a cinder block. He was so stocky, I bet he weighed about 250 pounds. James and I called him Mr. Fat. He was polite to my mother at first. He would bring over groceries and would visit her at least three times a week. He never said much to James or me other than hello.

Within a few months this seemingly pleasant guy went from being caring to callous and cruel. He became abusive toward my mother. I would hear them arguing. Then he would hit or choke her, and I could hear her in between breaths telling him, "Greg, please stop."

At the time Greg's scary behavior started, I was only nine years old. James was seven. All we could do was cover our ears and cry as we sat in the next room terrified for our mother. I was overwhelmed with the feeling of complete helplessness when my mother was being abused. Afterwards, I felt as if I should have done something to help her. James and I would talk about how we hated what he was doing to her, and we wished that he would just leave and never come back.

James said to me, "Man, why won't Mama just kick his ass, since she's taller than him?"

"The dude looks like a house," I replied. James fell silent.

Even at my young age, I realized that Greg's abuse of my mother was hurting James. I had been so worried about my mother at first that I'd overlooked the effect that all of this was having on my little brother. I saw the two of us as tough young men who had to protect our mother. The reality of it was that we were little kids and had to deal with our own pain caused by being unable to change things. We saw and heard our mother being physically and emotionally abused while we couldn't do anything to protect her. We went to bed many nights baffled, angry, and afraid.

The abuse continued off and on for almost a year. My brother and I were too young to understand why a man would physically abuse a woman and why a woman would stay in a relationship that was so toxic.

James would ask me, "Why is Mama still with him?"

"I have no idea," I would reply. I really didn't get it.

Then there came a day when I couldn't take it anymore. Greg hit my mother in front of me and I picked up a broom and swung it to hit him across his head. But he just swatted at me like I was an annoying fly. I fell to the floor, still full of rage, but more frightened.

Greg didn't live with us. He never took my mother out for dinner, a movie, or any place for that matter. His occasional grocery purchases for my mother had become almost nonexistent. In fact, he started to mooch. Greg was broke. As far as I could tell, he didn't have a bank account, credit card, or a car. James and I used to talk about how Greg was using our mother. Sure, our mother didn't have much, but Greg seemed to have even less.

I remember James saying, "I bet Greg doesn't even know how to drive."

"He's probably too short," I replied. James and I both laughed. Humor helped us get through the time of Greg.

My sister, Rhonda, was born in January. Rhonda was a pretty baby with longer hair than I thought she would have because my mother's hair wasn't long, and her father, Greg, had a receding hairline and not much hair. I noticed that people would stare openly at his unforgettable attempt at an Afro. I never understood why he didn't just cut off what little there was and please the crowds.

Syrup Sandwiches

With the addition of Rhonda, I started feeling like I had to step up and be the man of the house. I was only nine years old, but I felt like I had to protect both my brother and sister. My mother was struggling with a new baby and still being abused, and I felt a sense of responsibility for her too since I was the oldest. I knew that there wasn't much that I could do to protect my mother, but that didn't stop me from feeling like I had to. I would go to bed thinking about how I could make things better for my family. Of course, I was too young to be thinking like that. There wasn't much that I could realistically do that would make a big difference, but I knew that I had to at least try—there was no one else. Many nights I would lie awake thinking of ways to be more responsible than the father that had abandoned me. I resented not having a father and felt neglected. I felt that the only way that I could prove to my mother that I was reliable and responsible was to look after my brother and sister. Because no adult male had applied for the position, I convinced myself I had to be the family protector.

So now our family situation had gone from bad to worse. Even at that age I knew that my mother was lonely and needed some adult companionship, but did she really have to pick a man who would turn out to be another deadbeat dad? My mother had been struggling financially when she met Greg. I guess she thought that Greg would provide some measure of support. Wrong again! My mother used to tell James and me that Greg was "in between jobs." He wasn't working when they met. It's hard to be in between jobs when you didn't have a job in the first place. He was constantly "looking for work." Hell, even a blind squirrel can find an acorn occasionally. Why couldn't this grown ass man find any real work? Life is hard, but it's even harder if you're not motivated and persistent. I was a kid and had found work. I wondered if Greg could have seriously tried to find work.

Syrup Sandwiches

Chapter 6
Syrup Sandwiches

We had a limited supply of food. The truth is we went hungry a lot. The birth of Rhonda meant that we needed more money her for clothes, food, and baby stuff but there never seemed to be enough. My mother was on welfare and receiving government-funded food stamps in the middle of New York's fiscal crisis in the 1970s.

My mother would receive monthly food stamps in the amount of $154. These stamps came in booklets like coupon books and in denominations of $1, $5, and $10. The coupons were printed in brown, blue, and green respectively. We would use these stamps almost like cash. They could only be used to purchase uncooked food, so they could not be spent at restaurants.

There would be some store owners who would break the rules slightly and allow us to purchase cooked foods using food stamps. I think they felt bad for us. Besides, at the end of the day, the store owners would redeem the food stamps for cash, no matter what we bought as they did not have to provide that information.

Because my mother received food stamps and a welfare check monthly, she had to make sure that the food supply that we had lasted the entire month. It never did. James and I were two growing boys, and like most boys between the ages of eight and ten, we could often consume more groceries than were readily available.

When you don't have enough food, somehow, you become creative. James and I created quite a few sandwiches that you'd be hard-pressed to find in any deli in the city. Our earliest creation was the syrup sandwich. Any little kid can make it. I remember the first time I made a syrup sandwich. I poured the sticky Aunt Jemima Syrup on two pieces of bread and spread the syrup as evenly as I could with a butter knife, trying not to spill any. Then I made a sandwich by topping with the other slice of bread, and bit into what I thought was heaven. I fell in love with the sweet syrup and bread mix and washed it down with some cold water. Sure, it was only bread and syrup, but when there's nothing else to eat, almost anything tastes good.

The bread wasn't whole wheat bread. We had never heard of that. It was plain white bread. Not even Wonder Bread, which was one of the bestselling breads at that time, nor any other brand-name bread. The outside of the bread bag just read, "White Bread." The bread was so cheap, I don't think it had a company's name on the bag.

Besides the syrup sandwich, another Owens kid creation was the mayonnaise sandwich, which James hated. To this day, he can't stand mayonnaise. Yes, just mayo on bread. We had ketchup and mustard sandwiches too. But my favorite was the syrup sandwich.

Sometimes we had cereal and would have to eat it without milk because there was no milk available. Other times there was milk, but we had no cereal. We'd sometimes have powdered milk—just add water and you were good to go. On the rare occasions that we had both milk and cereal, those were good days. Rice was our go-to meal. We seemed to keep more rice than anything else even though that, too, often got low.

It was wonderful that my mother had gotten us our own apartment and that we weren't living with her brother and sister anymore. Although their apartment was in a brownstone and the second and third floors

Syrup Sandwiches

belonged to my Aunt Denise and Uncle Daniel, there was not enough space for three families with children on the first floor. We were living in close quarters with no privacy.

The new apartment in Bushwick was roomier, and since my mother didn't have much furniture, the rooms looked larger than they were. But we did have a bad problem that we didn't have in the brownstone. When you live in an apartment building, it's difficult to control the number of pests that seem to invade your apartment, namely roaches, mice, and sometimes rats. No matter how clean you keep your apartment, if your next-door neighbors have roaches, then you are more than guaranteed to have them too. I remember my mother contacting the landlord to ask him if he would fumigate the apartment for roaches and put down some boric acid and traps for the mice. The landlord, Mr. Schwartz, was an older white man, probably in his sixties. He was five foot six, and his round stomach made him appear much heavier than he probably was. His full beard was well trimmed, and he was well dressed like fashion was a priority. I think Mr. Schwartz liked my mother because he was forever kind to her and would smile from ear to ear whenever he saw her. He would pinch the cheeks on my face and say, "Hello, chubby face," whenever he saw me. I hated when he did that.

Mr. Schwartz owned more properties than the one we lived in and would go from property to property collecting rent. I used to imagine being wealthy like him. Eventually, Mr. Schwartz would accommodate my mother's request, after she spent weeks of waiting. The exterminator would come to the apartment and fumigate, lay some mice traps and boric acid, then tell us not to reenter the apartment for four to six hours. I think that the extermination process worked for three days, and then the roaches and mice were back all over the apartment again; and when they returned, it seemed as if they came back with their friends.

Part of the problem with the extermination process was that the landlord was too frugal to pay for all the apartments to be exterminated at the same time. When our apartment was getting fumigated, the pests left our apartment and went to our neighbors' apartments to hang out until it was safe for them to return to our apartment. We not only had regular roaches but also large water bugs or *black beetles* as they're sometimes called. These bugs were more difficult to get rid of than the regular roaches that were already as invincible as Superman. The pest problem didn't go away, and we got to a point where we got used to them. It wasn't like they were our friends or anything like that. I never stopped hating the mice and roaches. I would hear them running around in the kitchen at night and would feel disgusted. But we finally accepted that our efforts at ridding them were futile.

Both my mother and James had asthma and having an apartment full of roaches didn't help. They would often have trouble breathing, especially at night. I felt bad for them, but there was nothing that I could do other than get up at different times throughout the night and try to kill as many roaches as possible. I think the roaches slept during the day even though there were some stragglers that felt brave enough to chance crawling on the wall in the middle of the day right in front of me.

"The nerve of you bastards. Die, roach, die!" I'd shout at them, taking off my shoe—and splat!

The roaches didn't care if we had company over. I think they enjoyed watching us act as if we didn't see them. My mother used to feel bad about having bugs in the house and was concerned that people would see them and talk badly about her.

She would say, "People will think we are nasty if they see these roaches."

I told my mother, "Don't worry about what people say or think. Everyone that we know has roaches and mice too." And I think, for a short time, my pep talk worked.

Chapter 7
A Better Place

One sunny but cold morning, my brother and I were sitting on the fire escape talking about our fathers and trying to imagine how they looked. In particular, we wondered if we looked like them.

James said, "Man, I hope your dad looks better than you."

We both started laughing.

When we looked back down toward the street, there was this man, probably in his mid-forties, walking down the middle of the street. He was big and tall, easily six feet, four inches tall with big muscles. He looked like he lived at the gym. He was baldheaded with a big beard, but what made him stand out more than anything else was the fact that he was naked as a newborn baby. We looked at each other and then back at this man. I mean, what the hell were we watching? This man's penis was swinging from side to side as he walked proudly down the street. It was as if he owned Broadway Avenue and was informing everyone who didn't already know. I was only ten years old, and James was eight, so we were shocked to see a grown man naked with a penis that looked like it was too big for his body. Suddenly, three police officers came from out of nowhere and tackled him. They covered him with a blanket and hauled his crazy ass away in the patrol car. James and I had never heard of or seen anything like this. We later learned that the muscle-bound, naked man was a *streaker*. Well, damn! We laughed and talked about that for a long time. We later told our mother, and all she could do was shake her head. Knowing her, she probably wanted to see this streaker for herself.

In December, my mother was talking to my grandmother on the phone in what appeared to be a contentious conversation about something. I was eager to talk to my mother when she got off the phone to find out what all the quarreling was about. It was around the holiday season and my mother and grandmother were both watching the 1961 movie *King of Kings* with actor Jeffrey Hunter playing the role of Jesus. My mother and grandmother were going back and forth talking about the movie. My grandmother was telling my mother that the guy playing Jesus in the movie was really Jesus, and I could hear my mother telling her that he was just an actor and that he wasn't really Jesus. This went on for a while before they ended the call and said goodnight. My mother told me about the conversation, and I thought that was odd for my grandmother to think that the actor was God.

The next morning, my mother received a call from Aunt Lillie informing her that my grandmother had passed away. I can't describe the pain that I observed in my mother at the time—she appeared the saddest that I've ever seen.

I was ten years old, and had I just lost the only grandmother I knew. This was the first time that I had experienced dealing with death in the family. My mother was only twenty-nine years old, and she took her mother's death very hard. My grandmother was only fifty-five. I didn't know how to feel or how to deal with a loss of such magnitude. I felt bad that I had not had the opportunity to know my grandmother as well as I wished I could have.

She lived with my Aunt Lillie in Far Rockaway, a section of Queens, New York. This was far from us in Brooklyn, at least two or three different trains plus a bus ride. We didn't see our grandmother often, but when we did, I could feel the love she had for me and the rest of her grandchildren. When she spoke, she was soothing. She was a great listener, and she tried to be that rock that her children needed. I know that she dealt with pain and emotional suffering throughout her life: She dealt with the abuse from Oscar; the tragic death of her lover Nelson; and ten years before, when she was forty-five, she buried her twenty-six-year-old first child, Odessa. Now she was gone at fifty-five years of age. Life can be difficult to understand sometimes. My grandmother had to deal with so much. I thought, *Maybe, she is in a better place.*

What I remember of visits to my grandmother was her endless smile when she would tell me how tall I was getting. If James or I wanted some money to get some ice cream or candy, my grandmother would reach down into her bra, pull out her folded money, and give us a dollar. She'd remind us, "Don't eat too much sugar." James and I would smile as we ran out the door, both yelling, "OK, Grandma." The only real conversation I had with her was when I asked her about her parents. She mentioned something about slavery and didn't want to talk about it. I believe that maybe my great-grandparents may have been slaves or cotton pickers who were treated like slaves, and it was too difficult for her to discuss. I think the pain was so deep that she didn't want to relive all that she knew.

My mother had never told me that her father, Oscar, wasn't my Aunt Lillie's father. I learned that at my grandmother's funeral from Aunt Lillie. Oscar hadn't shown up to the funeral for the woman who gave him five children.

"Why didn't Grandpa show up?" I asked mother.

My mother whispered, "I don't know," then my Aunt Lillie, who was next to her, said, "To hell with him. He's not my father anyway."

I think my jaw dropped. I looked at my mother, and she turned her head as if to say, "Leave it alone." My aunt would later reveal to me that her real father was Nelson and tell the story of her parents' romance before Nelson's tragic death.

My mother was upset that her father didn't come to the funeral but tried not to show it. I knew that she was angry because after the funeral she said to no one in particular, "How dare he not show up." James and I looked at each other and just assumed that she was venting and said nothing.

After my grandmother passed away, I felt as if I didn't have any grandparents. I didn't know if I had any living grandparents on my father's side or if I'd ever meet them. Sure, I had Oscar for a grandparent, but this is the same man that neglected his children, abused the mother of his children, and chose not to build a solid relationship with any of his children, including my mother.

It was times like these when I needed someone other than my mother to talk with and to possibly help me deal with what I was going through. I felt my mother already had more on her plate than she could handle emotionally, financially, and physically without me adding to her worries. In addition to mourning for her mother and the endless battle to make ends meet, she had to deal with her boyfriend Greg's abuse and the accompanying stress. The sad part about not having someone educated and knowledgeable to talk with was that it forced me to figure out life's problems and issues on my own and without any help to avoid the many pitfalls that would undoubtedly come my way. I had to develop my own thought and healing processes as I grew and hoped that they would somehow work for me. Many times, I felt lost and didn't know how to find my way, but I knew that I had to appear strong and not let anyone see me struggling.

It was a typical Saturday evening around eight o'clock at night, and Greg and my mother could be heard arguing in the other room again.

"Get out! And don't put your hands on me again!" my mother yelled.

Greg didn't have a stuttering problem like my Sunday school teacher. However, he did have difficulty pronouncing my mother's name. Instead of calling her "Rena," he would say "Wena." He and the letter *r* didn't get along well. He also had a hard time trying to say any words that started with the letters *str:* The word *strawberry* became "scrawberry," and the word *straight* became "skrait."

I heard him yelling at her, "I ain't going nowhere, Wena!"

No sooner than he could finish messing up her name, there was a knock on the door to our apartment. I went to the door and looked through the peephole. On the other side stood a lady with an evil frown on her face. Her hair was standing up on her head like the Heat Miser at Christmas time.

She continued to knock on the door even as I asked, "Who is it?"

"Open the door, Greg! I know you're in there!"

Holy shit! This lady is asking for Greg, and his dumb ass is here arguing with my mother. I yelled for my mother to come to the door, and that's when Greg came running out of my mother's bedroom and into the room that James and I shared. Greg ran into the closet and hid. I guess he'd heard the lady's voice. It was sure loud enough.

My mother opened the door to the woman who was now screaming, "Where the hell is Greg? I know my husband's in here!"

Before my stunned mother could answer, I said, "He's in that room in the closet."

As I pointed the way, she ran past my mother and promptly dragged Greg's dumb ass out of the closet. Then, she kept pushing his back as you would push a person into a swimming pool. He resisted, as he didn't want to leave the apartment with her, but she was strong. I could see the fear on Greg's face, and I loved it. She pushed and pushed until he was out the front door.

As soon as they got into the hallway, she reached into her pocketbook and pulled out a long cooking knife. She proceeded to stab Greg repeatedly about the arms. After the stabbing, she turned around as if nothing just happened and walked down the stairs. That's when Greg ran back into our apartment with a trail of blood flowing from his arms and shoulders. He went into the kitchen and grabbed the five-pound bag of sugar that sat atop the cabinet and began pouring it into the open stab wounds. When the bleeding had stopped and his arms were draped with old T-shirts that were now too small for James and me, Greg left the apartment looking like a ghetto mummy. I wasn't sure where he went, but I doubt he went back home to his knife-wielding wife, at least not that night. He needed to go to the emergency room.

Shaking, my mother went to her room and cried herself to sleep.

I know she was surprised that Greg was married. She was upset that he lied about it and had fathered her third child. I wasn't happy that my mother had been deceived so badly, but I was elated to see the pain that was bestowed upon Dumb Ass from the hands of his wife. He was lucky that 'Wena' hadn't jumped in and kicked his ass too. They say that sometimes good things can come from a bad situation. I felt like Greg being married was a bad thing for my mom, but the good that came from it was that he was gone. *Bye-bye, Greg,* or so I thought.

We hadn't seen Greg for about two months, and suddenly, out of nowhere, this jerk shows up like roaches at nighttime. I guess that he and my mother were still communicating during his physical absence. She gave in to his begging and pleading and believed that he and his wife were no longer living together. He knocked on the door, out of breath after walking up four flights of stairs. He was holding a bag of groceries and had an awkward smile on his face like he was forced to show his crooked, missing, and stained teeth.

He said, "Hello, boys," to me and James. We looked at each other as if to say, "What in the hell is he doing here?" Neither of us said anything as he pushed his stocky ass past us and went into the kitchen to place the grocery bag on the table.

I called for my mother to tell her that Greg was here. When she came out of the room, hand-in-hand with Rhonda, my little sister, she didn't seem surprised but rather happy to see him. It was at that point that I knew she had forgiven him. It was hard for me to totally understand why my mother was so weak for Greg when he was abusive and already married.

I think that if she had had a father who had cared for her mother, her expectations of men might have been different. Each time I saw something like this happening, I told myself that I can't be like that. Every time I saw something that I knew was not right, it only solidified my determination to do and be better. I was determined not to be like Greg, or my grandfather, or my uncles or my

Syrup Sandwiches

dad. They didn't show my mother what to look for in a man. They didn't show me how to be a man. But they did show me that being like them wasn't an option.

I could see in my mother how the abandonment and lack of nurturing and love from her father had formed not only her expectations of male partners but her view of fathers. I remember one time James asked our mother, "Mom, do you think we need our fathers?"

Without blinking an eye my mother replied, "Y'all don't need no fathers—I am your mother and father!"

James and I didn't have many friends, but we did befriend two other boys our age, Eric and Keith. They were brothers, and unlike James and me, they both shared the same father, but he was not present in their lives either. I remember Eric saying, "Let's get into some mischief." Now his definition of mischief was different than mine, but James and I followed along anyway. Next thing we knew, we were walking miles and miles to different libraries to see if we could take books from the library without getting caught. That's right, our mischief consisted of stealing books from the library. The sad thing about the insanity was that we never read the books that we stole. Talk about dumb. We would walk up to forty city blocks, which is about four miles, and go into the library just to steal a book. It was times like this that I wish we had a father or some other adult with some common sense who could have pulled us aside and told our dumb asses to stop the madness, to take the books back, and to never do it again. Unfortunately, we didn't have that. We finally stopped stealing the books, not because we got caught but because we realized it was pointless. Those long walks were wearing out our sneakers, and we didn't have the money to replace them like we wanted.

My mother never sat me or James down and had a heart-to-heart talk about girls, life, money, or anything for that matter. I think that my mother didn't know how to effectively communicate with two growing boys. My mother told me that she and her mother used to talk all the time about almost everything. I believe that a relationship between a mother and a daughter is vastly different than a relationship between a mother and a son. I can understand how difficult it might have been for my mother to share her deepest thoughts with James and me and to discuss our personal concerns at length. This gap in her parenting skills made our fatherlessness more of an issue. I was determined that if I ever had children, I would make sure that I consistently communicated with them and prepared them for life's journey. My mother was young and was still growing up, just as James and I were.

Chapter 8
Fire Escape

One thing about sitting on the fire escape, we didn't have to worry about anyone bothering us. We had a bird's eye view of the people below, and they didn't see us nestled in the fire escape four stories above them. But one Saturday, when I was eleven and James was nine, we found our invisibility threatened. We were out there around seven in the evening enjoying the warm breeze and brotherly conversation. I remember James was telling me one of the girls in his class liked him. Then, midstory, he stopped. Below us, two guys were coming into our building. They were carrying what looked like a tool bag. We'd never seen them before, and they were looking over their shoulders as they entered the building.

As soon as they got into the building, we heard banging. I dialed 911 and told the dispatcher, "I think someone is breaking into the apartment downstairs."

I gave them my name and address, and surprisingly, the police came quickly. It was odd for the police to respond to any calls from our neighborhood in a timely manner. Often when the police were called, they didn't show up until thirty minutes later. I was glad they showed up when they did and had sent two patrol cars. Next thing I knew, the police escorted the two criminals out of the building in handcuffs. As I watched them putting the men into the patrol cars, I saw one of the men looking up at James and me. My heart stopped beating for a second in fear of this criminal looking at us and knowing that one of us probably called the cops. I didn't sleep well that night, and it wasn't because of the trains. I was visibly shaken by the look that criminal in the back seat of the police car had given me, as if he was looking at me thoroughly so he wouldn't forget my face.

In Brooklyn in the 1970s, there were places throughout the city, normally schools or churches, where people who were homeless or on welfare could go and get free food. Many of these places would distribute commodities - blocks of processed cheese, powdered milk, powdered eggs, beans, canned processed meats, and rice. One Thursday, around 4:30 in the evening, my mother went to get some free groceries. James and I had already arrived home from school earlier and had finished our homework. Our mother made sure that we did our homework before we did anything else, and I am so grateful she did. We loved to get our homework done because then we could go outside and play.

We decided that it was fire escape time, so we went outside and began talking it up as usual. I wanted to know all about the girl who had a crush on my little brother. When I asked James about Karen, he said, "Man, she only wanted to get to know me so that I could introduce her to my friend Paul." I said, "Damn, that's messed up." I was upset that my little brother was used like that.

As we looked over the sets of train tracks, we could see our mother pushing her shopping cart with the free groceries. As she was nearing our apartment, two women approached her and tried to take her food. A scuffle ensued, and she fought with them for what seemed like ten minutes. I could see her defending herself as best as possible as the women were swinging and punching at her, trying to get her to release her shopping cart. But my mother wouldn't let go, and as

Syrup Sandwiches

other people approached, the would-be robbers ran off with what little food they could carry. My mother demonstrated then—as she had so many times—that she wasn't a quitter.

"Never give up on anything that you want in life," she constantly told James and me.
"Quitting is easy. Don't take the easy way out."

It was a terrible feeling watching our mother being attacked and not being able to do anything about it. But I was glad that she stood up to those thieves. When she finally made it home, I didn't see any bruises or cuts on her, but she was visibly shaken.

I said, "Rena, we saw what happened. Are you OK?"

As usual, she said, "I'm fine." Whenever she said, "I'm fine," that told me that she was handling it.

The next day, my mother sat me down to talk with me. She said "Anthony, you don't have to worry about me. I need you to stay focused on school."

"I'm not worried about you," I lied. "I just don't want anyone to hurt you."

"I realize that you are starting to grow up and trying to become a man, but I can take care of myself," she said. Hearing that she noticed I was becoming a man, I beamed with joy. Since I was the oldest male in the house, I had to act like I was the man of the house even though I was only eleven.

You've probably been wondering why I am allowed to get away with calling my mother "Rena" and not "Mom" or "Mother" like James and Rhonda did. People often asked, and still ask, "Why do you call your mother 'Rena'?"

I tell them, "Because that's her name."

I have never been disrespectful to my mother, and if she would have wanted me to call her "Mom" or "Mother," then I would have easily done so. My mother allowed me to call her "Rena" and didn't have a problem with it. She was good with it, so was I. To this day, I still call her by her birth name. My brother and sister used to think that I was getting special treatment because I am the oldest. That wasn't the case.

One thing about being in any part of New York during the winter is that the chance of getting snow was almost guaranteed, and I'm not talking about a few inches or a foot. There were times when we had so much snow that shovels were a waste of time. New York is well equipped to deal with snowstorms and severe weather. For the city to shut down public transportation, which includes the city buses and trains, there must be a significant amount of snow accumulation. When public transportation shuts down, that normally means all the city schools will be closed as well for snow days.

My brother and I attended public elementary schools in Brooklyn. There were private schools in our area, but my mother couldn't afford any of them, not while being on welfare. New York has five boroughs: Brooklyn, which is the largest; Queens; the Bronx; Manhattan; and Staten Island. At the time, they all had public schools that were numbered from one up to any three-digit number, and those numbers could be the same in different boroughs. There could be a Public School Eleven (PS 11) in the Bronx and another Public School Eleven (PS 11) in Queens. There were intermediate, middle, junior, and of course, high schools. My first school was Public School Five (PS 5), which accommodated students who were pre-kindergarten through the fifth grade.

I remember going to school hungry many days because our pantry—I mean *cabinet*—was completely empty. The school provided free breakfast and lunch for children whose families could not afford it, and that was

Syrup Sandwiches

one of the reasons why I enjoyed going to school, in addition to learning new things and meeting new friends. I was in the fifth grade when I got into my first kerfuffle. This girl who was in my class didn't like me, and one day she said, "I don't like your big head." I thought, my head doesn't look that big. I said to her, "So—I don't care." Next thing I knew, she leaned over to me and bit the shit out of me on my right arm. Before long, I was in the school nurse's office. The nurse called my mother to come pick me up and take me home. I was really upset that I had to go home because this happened early in the morning right after breakfast; and because I had to go home, I knew that I would miss the school's lunch. I was really mad at that little heifer.

    Since we could not afford toys like other children our age who had a family with two incomes, we relied on free games that we could play outside, such as, spinning tops, tag, hide-and-seek, and skelly. Back then, we would go outside and play all day, unlike kids today who are captivated by computers and tablets. We played and had fun until the sun had gone completely down and until we could barely see our hands in front of our faces because of the darkness. We'd play with the same children that lived on our block and would often meet them after we did our homework. We all were so used to hanging out together that if any of us didn't show up to play, one of us would go to their apartment to see what the problem was.

    I remember one time when one of our friends didn't show up to play. I went to his apartment to see if he would be coming out, and his mother said, "Bobby can't come outside because he got into trouble at school today." I knew better than to ask what he did, so I replied, "Thanks, Ms. Smith," and ran back outside to share the news with the crew.

Although Bushwick had a lot of crime, we stayed outside and played, not worrying about any danger. We just had fun playing. One thing about playing outside, we were near the apartment; and whenever our mother wanted us for anything, she would stick her head out of the window and yell our names: "James, come inside!" or just, "Anthony!" We knew then we had to stop what we were doing and go inside to see what she needed, thinking it was something important. Usually, it wasn't. We would run inside only to be told to take the trash out or to stay inside to look after our baby sister, Rhonda. During this time, our mother would go to the store for some more milk or baby food. Whenever my mother yelled *my* name out of the window, for some reason it always seemed louder, maybe because my name had more syllables than James's. Hell, I don't know why, but it sure was annoying.

It seemed like she wanted me just when I was having the most fun, like when we were playing with our spinning tops. Spinning tops were made in the sixties and seventies and were diamond shaped and normally made from wood. They had a sharp point on the bottom that would allow them to spin in a circle after they were flung from your hands. The tops would have a string that wrapped around the spinning top that created a spinning action when the top was flung. Most of the tops were made by a company named Duncan.

These were like the fidget spinners kids use today. But with the spinning tops, you would throw them toward the ground much like you would a dart, while clutching the top's string in your hand. Today, fidget spinners are sometimes used to help people who have trouble focusing or may need help with anxiety or psychological stress. Some say the fidget spinner can help those with attention deficit hyperactivity disorder (ADHD) or autism. I don't know if our spinning tops

Syrup Sandwiches

helped with stress or any psychological disorders, but they sure were fun.

By far, our most exhausting outside game was tag. The objective of tag was to get other players 'out' by chasing and then touching (called tagging) them. After a person was tagged, we would say, "Tag, you're it." The last person tagged was the "it" person for the next round. We would play tag for what seemed like hours, only to be drenched with sweat and too tired to walk up the stairs to our apartment. Playing tag helped me develop my quickness and elusiveness, which I would later need while defending myself in high school. In the game of hide-and-seek, the person chosen as "it" would close their eyes, count to ten, and then would say, "Ready or not, here I come." Then they would attempt to find all the hidden players. Since we lived in a small apartment, hiding inside our apartment didn't work very well because the only hiding spots we had were the closet, bathroom, or under the bed. So, we played outside and would hide behind or under parked vehicles, behind trees, or several other locations. Oftentimes, the "it" person would give up because they were unable to find us.

Skelly (some call it skully or scully) was by far my favorite outside game. There would be a group of at least six of us, all boys between the ages nine to fourteen, and we'd all meet after school. Skelly was played on the actual tar streets in Brooklyn and throughout New York. To play it, you'd draw a large square box, usually with chalk. Inside this box were smaller square boxes that were numbered from one to twelve. In the center of all these squares was one larger box that contained the number thirteen. To play the game you had to have some type of bottle cap or any small, round object that was heavy yet could easily glide across the street's tar surface. The cap was usually filled with wax, tar, or dirt to make it heavy enough to knock other players' caps out of the box you were trying to get into. The objective of the game was to use your cap to get from box number one to box number thirteen in order, but you could get set back. If your cap was knocked out of any of the boxes, you'd have to start all over. The winner was the one whose cap landed in box thirteen first. This game would take hours because we would have to stop the game every time a vehicle passed.

We really looked forward to going outside. We hated when it rained because we had to stay inside, and not having any games or toys to play with made for a long day or night. Luckily for us, we did have an old yo-yo that we found in one of the closets when we moved into the apartment. Apparently, the yo-yo dates to 440 BC—ours was not that old. We would play with this yo-yo when we had to stay inside because of the weather. We would try to perform various tricks with the yo-yo, like "walk the dog," "rock the baby," or "around the world." James was much better with the yo-yo than I.

Life is like a yo-yo. There are fun and games, and then harsh reality snaps back with a vengeance. I will never forget one dark and freezing January morning when something alerted my unconscious mind and snapped me awake from my sleep. It was 1:30 a.m. and I could hear the gasps for air that were coming from my mother's room. This wasn't unusual. Her asthma, more severe than James's, often bothered her at night but I rarely woke up from the sounds. Then a tremendous thump startled me. Hearing another and another, I sat up—someone was banging on our apartment door so loudly that I thought the door would give way. A deep voice yelled, "Get out! There's a fire!" and immediately I jumped out of bed. I shook James and said, "Get up, James. There's a fire!"

James and I ran into our mother's room. As James was waking my mother, I was picking Rhonda up out of bed. James and I already had on pajamas that we slept in every night, and only smelling light smoke and knowing it would be freezing outside, we chanced the time putting on our shoes and coats. I put Rhonda's coat on her and wrapped her in a blanket. I could see the apartment building adjacent to ours was engulfed in flames. We hoped ours hadn't yet been ignited but didn't take time to grab anything of value, not that we really had anything valuable. Maybe we would have saved some food stamps and some baseball cards that my brother and I collected if we'd dared. But I could smell the smoke intensifying and couldn't think of anything but safely escaping. Rhonda was sobbing and trembling. My mother was panicking and screaming.

People were all running to exit the building at the same time. Some people were carrying suitcases, and I saw someone carrying a small television. I could not believe my eyes. *The damn building was on fire, and you are worried about a TV. Wow!*

There was so much confusion and panic as the smoke started to fill our apartment building. Someone ran into me so hard I almost dropped Rhonda. People were yelling and screaming as they scurried toward the exit. I ran down the stairs, flight after flight, holding Rhonda in my arms like she was a baby, with James and my mother in tow. Now the fire had quickly spread into our building and had engulfed the three apartments of the adjacent building that were closest to the fire.

We were terrified. As the smoke started to slowly fill our nostrils and lungs, our panic grew. I was only eleven, James was nine, and Rhonda had just turned three. We were competing with large adults to get out of the building. I wasn't sure if we would make it out safely, as people were falling over each other as they were trying to get to the exit. We covered our mouths and nostrils in order to protect ourselves from the dense smoke that had blanketed our apartment building while at the same time trying to take in enough air to breathe.

I can close my eyes now as an adult and remember that awful smell – burning wood, melting electrical wire, and burning furniture from the apartment building. We finally made it to the exit. James was mature for his age at nine and didn't panic even as he and my mother narrowly escaped the falling embers and crumbling ceiling, which had nearly fallen directly on their heads as they passed through the doorway. I was so proud of my brother.

We stood outside in the freezing cold in the middle of winter, shivering and afraid, watching the firemen battle this enormous blaze. I looked over at my mother, and all I could see were tears streaming down her face. It was hard for me not to cry. I told myself that I had to be strong and not let my family see me crying too. I was the self-appointed man of the house, and I had to do everything that I could to appear as strong as possible even in the face of despair.

We stood outside in the freezing cold for about five hours before the firemen allowed us to return to our apartment building to recover any possession that we could. Luckily, the fire had only impacted the three apartments in our building that were closest to the building that initially caught fire. Our apartment wasn't damaged by the fire, but due to the severity and damage to the other apartments, in the end, the building was uninhabitable.

The cause of the fire was determined to be a kerosene heater which had been inadvertently tipped over. Back then, many people used kerosene heaters to provide additional warmth since the radiators were often inadequate. When winter temperatures in New York

Syrup Sandwiches

dipped down to the single digits, one or two radiators in an apartment weren't adequate to keep a family warm. There were many kerosene fires in New York during the cold winters. Kerosene heaters could kill in another way too. Many years later, my cousin Annette would die in her New York apartment from carbon monoxide poisoning from a kerosene heater. We had one kerosene heater, but for better or worse, most of the winter we didn't have enough money to buy kerosene to put into it.

Although the fire had never directly made it to our home on the fourth floor, the smoke made it smell as if everything in our rooms had been burned. My mother told us to pack some clothes. We were going to go and stay with her sister Denise for a few days so that the apartment could air out. There was only one suitcase in the house, and my mother packed it with her and Rhonda's clothing. James and I used garbage bags to pack our clothes. It was around seven o'clock in the morning when we all were ready to go to my aunt's house. My mother, James, Rhonda, and I walked for three miles to the Fort Green section of Brooklyn where my Aunt Denise lived. We stayed with her for a week before returning home.

Chapter 9
Pitkin Avenue

Aunt Denise was my mother's oldest living sister and was married to a man named Travis. She was about five feet, seven inches tall and weighed around 185 pounds. When she walked, her feet turned out and her toes were farther apart than her ankles, which made her walk like a duck. Aunt Denise wore glasses and relied heavily on her bifocals to function. Her vision was severely diminished without her glasses, and she would sometimes misplace them.

I remember one time she asked James and me to help her find her glasses. She never called us by our names. She would say, "You boys, your aunt has lost her glasses again. Please help me find them."

James and I searched her entire apartment before we located her glasses underneath her bed. I wondered how they got under the bed and whether one pair of glasses was enough. Then there was another time when she needed help finding her glasses, and we found them in the trash. James and I thought that maybe she was putting something in the trash when they fell off her face and then she somehow became distracted and didn't remember them falling. The last time that she asked James and me to help her find her glasses, we let her search her apartment over and over until she sat down, exhausted. Then James said, "Aunt Denise, your glasses are on top of your head." James and I knew they were there the entire time, but we wanted to have some fun. I

Syrup Sandwiches

hope that if I ever need to wear glasses, I can keep up with them. I can see how much of a problem it can be if you need your glasses and you can't find them.

Denise only had one child, Kem, who was in the Army and stationed in Germany. Kem was five years older than I. I would sometimes see him when he would return home to visit his mother. Kem was Aunt Denise's pride and joy. He could do no wrong. She would tell us how great a kid he was and how proud she was of him for going into the Army and doing something with his life. Aunt Denise provided emotional support to my mother and would try to help her financially whenever she could by giving her food or sometimes a buck or two to help her stretch her welfare check. Denise was frugal when it came to money, I mean, she held on to a dollar so tightly that you'd have to pry it out of her hands with a crowbar. I think that in some ways Aunt Denise felt sorry for my mother, who now had three children. Sometimes I would see my aunt and mother talking, and Denise would often give her a look of pity. I was over at my aunt's house one day, and I wanted to get some candy from the corner store.

I said, "Aunt Denise, may I have a quarter, please, to get some candy?"

"No! I'm not giving you any money." It was the way that she said "no" that made me feel like it would be very wise to never ask her for money again. I was only eight years old when I asked for a quarter, and I never asked her for any money again.

But Denise was great at hosting and was a good cook, so we looked forward to eating at her house—that is, when *she* was cooking. Her husband, Travis, liked to cook too, but his food tasted as if he had poured an entire box of salt into it. I'm not talking about fancy salt like pink Himalayan, Kosher, sea salt, or even Morton's. I'm talking about plain old cheap salt. That salt was so terrible that they were practically giving it away in the stores. The stores were so happy to get rid of that cheap salt that if you'd buy the salt, they'd give you the pepper free. Uncle Travis loved that salt. I remember seeing him pour some of that cheap salt on a small mountain of snow and watching the snow melt away like a hot knife to butter.

    I remember one of the few family holiday parties we had was at my Aunt Denise's. I must have been thirteen. She invited my mother, Aunt Lillie, her brother Daniel, and all the children. Aunt Denise and Uncle Travis lived in a brownstone, so they had enough room for large gatherings. When I walked into the house, the fantastic aroma of some of her renowned dishes hit me. I suspect that she had to let Uncle Travis do some of the cooking too. It smelled like I had walked into a restaurant and bakery at the same time. All I could think about was eating—that's when I noticed that the table was set beautifully, and it looked like something on television. I noticed there were napkins, forks, knives, and spoons meticulously placed about the table.

    My aunt pointed to a table that looked like a card table and told us children, "The grownups will be eating at the main table, and you all will be eating at the table over there." The table was not fancy at all, just set with paper napkins, plastic forks, knives, and spoons. But I was too hungry to care about cutlery. I was only concerned about eating.

    After we all held hands and my aunt said a prayer to bless the food, it was time to eat—that's when Uncle Daniel decided to show up. Daniel is my mother's second oldest brother and a spitting image of his father, my grandfather. Not only was he late but he came to dinner smelling like he had climbed out of an alcohol barrel. Any open flame could have quickly set my drunk uncle ablaze. After a few tense words between him and

Syrup Sandwiches

Aunt Denise, we all began to eat. I thought everything was fine until my drunk uncle started fussing with Uncle Travis. The arguing became so intense that Uncle Travis had to kick Uncle Daniel out of the house. Even drunk, Uncle Daniel probably knew that he shouldn't entice Uncle Travis into a fight. Travis was twice his size. So, Daniel had to leave without finishing dinner. After all the commotion was over, the rest of us enjoyed dessert.

Aunt Denise and Uncle Travis didn't stay a couple. My mother told me that Uncle Travis would often bloody Aunt Denise's nose or choke her until she passed out. He would yell at her and tell her how stupid she was. Uncle Travis didn't care who was around when he berated her. I heard his rants a few times myself. I felt terrible for her. I'm not sure if they got divorced or not, but my mother told me that they were no longer together. I guess my aunt got sick and tired of his maltreatment. In Brooklyn back then, most people didn't get divorced. They just went their separate ways.

For the life of me, I could not figure out why men—I mean grown boys like Travis and Greg—would rather physically abuse the women in their lives, who did anything and everything for them, instead of loving them and supporting them. Travis died some years after he and Aunt Denise went their separate ways. He had high blood pressure, diabetes, and a long list of other serious issues. I think it was the salt.

I can count on three fingers the number of families that we knew that had both a husband and wife: There was Aunt Denise and Travis for a while; my cousin, Howard, and his wife, Priscilla; and Aunt Lillie and her husband, Lewis.

My mother's cousin Howard was the only one in the entire family who had any money. I mean, he and Priscilla both had full-time jobs and were nearing retirement age. Plus, they owned a beautiful, two-story brownstone in the East New York section of Brooklyn. Howard bought a new car every year. He loved Cadillacs and would drive over to our apartment sometimes, I think, just to show off his latest purchase. I don't ever remember him coming upstairs into the apartment to sit down and talk with my mother or any of us. He worked as an electrician at a major electrical company. He was one of the supervisors and had been there for almost thirty years. His wife, Priscilla, was the human resources supervisor at a large and successful textile company.

I would call Howard from time to time to say hello and to see how he was doing. We never had any heart-to-heart talks or shared anything other than small talk. I enjoyed seeing and talking with Howard, but I felt as if he didn't want to talk about anything other than himself or his cars, which he loved so much. I found it disheartening that I couldn't share with him how I needed someone to confide in and depend on for some adult male guidance. Howard wasn't physically abusive toward his wife, as far as I knew, but he loved to drink. His favorite was Johnny Walker Scotch. Howard was a functional alcoholic. He could easily go to work early in the morning after a night of heavy drinking. There wasn't a time that I didn't see Howard intoxicated. He had alcohol before work. I'm not sure if he drank on the job, but I know he had some spirits after work, and a night cap wasn't out of the realm of possibilities. When he retired, his drinking went from bad to constant.

I remember James and I were walking down Pitkin Avenue, which is in an area of Brooklyn called East New York. Pitkin Avenue was a scaled-down shopping district. The stores sold food, shoes, clothing, furniture, and almost anything you could imagine. There were no high-end stores like Macy's or Dillard's, but they had local stores owned by people of various nationalities. You could haggle with most of them for

Syrup Sandwiches

lower prices. As we were walking, James and I saw a car parked with its passenger door open. This seemed odd to us as Pitkin Avenue was normally bustling with shoppers and would-be criminals venturing to rob someone or one of the many stores. We looked in the car, and in the driver's seat we saw our cousin Howard passed out. I knew he was drunk because I could smell the alcohol permeating from the passenger side. It was one o'clock in the afternoon, and it was a hot and muggy day. The temperature was expected to be in the upper nineties.

"Howard, wake up," I said repeatedly.

It was only after I went over to the driver's side that I saw that he was knocked out like a Mike Tyson opponent. I shook him several times before he would regain consciousness. When he woke up, he looked confused as if he was wondering, *'Who am I? Who parked this car? What came first, the chicken or the egg?'*

He was finally able to ask, "What are you boys doing here?"

"We're just walking around and looking," I said. We were window shopping, looking at all the things that we didn't have and hoped we could buy one day. We often shopped like that to break the monotony of being in the house.

Howard then straightened the hat on his head, and without even a goodbye to us, started his car, and drove off. It's amazing that he never killed anyone or himself driving drunk.

Howard's wife, Priscilla, was just as evil as Little-Bit. No, I take that back—she was worse. She was the bourgeois evil lady who had the money to back up her self-proclaimed privilege. Priscilla was mean to everyone all the time, except me. For some strange reason she was friendly to me. I think it was because I'd built a relationship with her when I would call from time to time to speak to Howard. She and I would have brief conversations on the phone before I spoke with her husband. She would ask about school or how I was doing.

I wasn't afraid of Priscilla as my mother and everyone else was. Priscilla would put a person in their place if they said anything that she didn't like, and she didn't care how they felt about her verbal lashing. It seemed as if people were afraid to talk to her because they feared her wrath. It never bothered me. I think Priscilla was a warmhearted person inside; she was just misunderstood. People misjudged her because of her straightforwardness. I would go over to visit them when I could, and I felt that Priscilla liked it that I wasn't intimidated by her and her sometimes dark and callous disposition.

I would guess that Priscilla acted that way because her husband was a drunk and she couldn't deal with the fact that she couldn't control him as she did everyone else in her life. Priscilla loved Howard, and it was obvious that she didn't like for him to drink or get drunk as often as he did. Many times, I heard Priscilla say to Howard, "You need to stop drinking so much." Howard acted as if he didn't hear her or would merely respond, "OK." Whenever he got drunk around her in public, she became irritated and would immediately tell him that she wanted to go home. Her efforts to curb or reduce Howard's drinking were futile, and of course, Priscilla didn't like that.

Howard wasn't physically abusive toward Priscilla, but I can see how emotionally challenging it must have been for her to have to deal with someone who had reached such a level of self-destruction and wasn't willing to seek any counseling or help to get better. Howard continued to function in his daily life as if nothing was wrong. However, his health was rapidly deteriorating. He kept his health status private, and the news of his death was a shock to all of us except his immediate family. Howard died from cirrhosis of the liver at fifty-eight years of age. I took his death hard because we had a relationship. Even though it wasn't as substantive as I needed, he was still someone that I looked up to as far as being a hardworking man who provided for his family. Although Howard had a problem with alcohol, I still saw that he worked to ensure that his family didn't have to do without the things that they needed. His death showed me how precious and short life could be and reinforced in my mind that I wouldn't waste my life on things that might interfere with my one day being the best father that I could be. Howard didn't know it, but I learned valuable life lessons from him that helped me reach my goals in life such as nothing in life comes easy and working hard has its benefits. But more importantly, I learned that providing for your family includes not only monetary assets but being emotionally available.

Chapter 10
Trendsetter

My Aunt Lillie, whom I will always love as a mother, was my mother's closest friend and sibling. She was born four years after my mother. Lillie had two children, both girls, Julie and Annette. Julie and I are the same age, and Annette and James are the same age. It appeared that my mother and Lillie planned the naming of their children so that the girls and boys would have the same first letter in their first names: Anthony and James; Annette and Julie. If it wasn't planned, it was a hell of a coincidence.

Aunt Lillie was a trendsetter and when she had her mind set on doing something, she would not let anything get in her way or stop her. She was attractive, about five foot seven and 135 pounds. When she walked into a room, her slim figure and beautiful smile often turned heads.

I viewed Aunt Lillie as the smart one. She had more worldly experiences than anyone else that I knew. Aunt Lillie loved adventure and a good challenge. She pursued a career in modeling and acting and landed a few acting roles, mostly in commercials. She loved modeling and would perform as a runway model in fashion shows. Her modeling and acting career never got to the level that she wanted, and her bills still needed to be paid, so she started driving the bus for the public schools in Manhattan.

Lillie was a great seamstress and could sew practically anything she wanted to from wedding gowns to men's pants. She was very good at it; I often asked her why she didn't sew for a living. She would say, "I love sewing. It's my hobby but not my career."

When I made money from packing grocery bags at the grocery store or getting paid from my summer jobs that were provided by the city, I would go to the fabric store and purchase five yards of material and a pattern, and my Aunt Lillie would sew pants for me with any design that I wanted. My favorite pants were a pair of black polyester slacks that had the standard zipper, but they also had a horizontal zipper for the right and left pockets with a gold button just above the zippers. The pants fit perfectly and accentuated my slender six-foot, five-inch frame. One thing I liked more than anything was the fact that I could have zippers and buttons anywhere I liked. These pants weren't like the ones that you could purchase in any store—they had extra designs, better fabric, and you could tell immediately that they were tailor-made. I felt special when my aunt would hand sew my clothes. I was in heaven when I wore them. It was awesome.

Lillie sewed clothing for herself, her children, and anyone who would ask. She was so giving and sweet, but at the same time she didn't take any mess from anyone. She wasn't a pushover, and no man would ever lay a hand on her. That's the reason why she and her husband, Lewis, separated. Lewis became emotionally abusive, and then he tried to physically assault her.

I remember asking my cousin Julie, "Why did your father leave?"

"Anthony, my mother had to leave Lewis," she asserted. "She wasn't going to let him hit her."

I was so happy to hear that my aunt had stood up to Lewis. Right away, I thought that if my mother, my grandmother, and my Aunt Denise would have stood up to their abusers, their lives could have been different. I responded to Julie with a grin, "Damn right."

Julie laughed. My aunt wouldn't let anyone abuse her and she wouldn't back down from anyone, especially if she felt that she was being treated unfairly or spoken to in an appropriate way. She wasn't afraid of anyone or anything, except animals that had teeth.

I remember her telling me, "Anthony, I don't get along well with animals that have teeth."

I asked, "Why not?"

"If they have teeth, they can bite," she replied. All I could do was smile and agree with her. If a dog was coming her way, she would cross the street to get away from it whether the dog was on a leash or not.

Lillie was an excellent cook, and I learned a great deal about cooking from her. She made the best sweet potato pie that I've ever tasted. She would go into the kitchen and pour herself a glass of red wine, usually a Cabernet Sauvignon. Then she would begin to cook up her masterpieces. I remember being at her house when she was baking some meatloaf, cabbage, and macaroni and cheese. She showed me the ingredients as she was mixing them with the ground beef for the meatloaf. She said, "Anthony, when you cook, you have to take your time. You can't rush because if you mess up the food, you might as well throw it away."

She lived in Far Rockaway, Queens for many years with my grandmother and would eventually move to Manhattan. Often Lillie came to visit my mother in our Bushwick apartment. One day, she came to the window that led to the fire escape, stuck her head out the window, and said to James and me, "Do you all have enough room for me?"

James and I laughed so hard just imagining her trying to get out of the window to sit on the fire escape.

Syrup Sandwiches

I jokingly said, "Yes. Come on out here." We knew she was only kidding. It was her witty and fun personality that I loved so much.

Aunt Lillie and my cousin, Howard, were the only ones who had vehicles while I was growing up. My aunt had an orange Volkswagen Beetle—yes, orange! Whenever she said that she would come over to visit with us and to take us for a ride, James and I would sit out on the fire escape for what seemed like hours waiting on her. I remember one time we waited so long that the sun went down. We got tired of waiting on the fire escape and went inside only to stare out the window. We watched each car that approached and passed the building, hoping that the next car would be Lillie's.

Eventually, Lillie showed up with Annette and Julie in the car. Our eyes lit up. "Mom, Mom, Aunt Lillie is here!" James called.

My mother had my sister ready to go, and of course, James and I had been ready for hours. We headed downstairs to get into the Orange Bug. We appreciated having someone in our family who was willing to spend some quality time with us. There was no one else in the entire family who spent more time with my mother and us than my Aunt Lillie.

At twelve, I already imagined being able to drive a car like my aunt did. But I hoped to get a better car. My aunt's Volkswagen had a hole in the rear floorboard. As she drove down the street, you could see the asphalt. The hole started out about the size of a golf ball and eventually grew to the size of a tennis ball.

As we were getting into the Orange Bug, Julie got out of the front passenger seat so that my mother could sit up front. James, Annette, Julie, Rhonda, and I sat in the back seat. It was a tight fit even for two twelve-year-olds, two ten-year-olds, and a three-year-old. Once when we were packed in the back seat, it started to rain.

As the rain continued to come down, my aunt tried to avoid as many puddles in the street as possible, swerving from left to right, trying to keep us in the back from getting wet. When it rained, the hole in the floorboard allowed the water to splash into the car and soak its back seat passengers. We sat back there smiling as if we were on an amusement park ride. But next thing we knew, she hit a big puddle of water, and we all got soaked. There was only so much she could do to keep us dry because there was too much traffic for her to avoid all the puddles. Sometimes we would get to our destination wetter than if we would have walked with an umbrella.

We enjoyed the forty-five-minute ride to Far Rockaway; it wasn't like riding on the subway and buses for hours and dealing with the crowds. Lillie was kindhearted to almost everyone and over the years would open her apartment to many children in need by becoming a foster parent. I remember her being a foster parent to a brother and sister and then again to a little girl. She treated the foster children just like she treated her own children. She showed them kindness, provided discipline, and most of all, unconditional love. I learned a lot from her and seeing how she gave love to children who weren't her own warmed my heart. I hoped to one day be as loving and thoughtful as she was. I saw in her a strong person who knew how to care, share, and demand respect.

Far Rockaway, Queens was different from Brooklyn. There seemed to be more trees, parks, and better homes in Far Rockaway. Everything just seemed cleaner. It was almost like being in another state. It was like going from an abandoned building into a luxury penthouse. Had it not been for the tall apartment buildings, one would wonder whether it really was part of New York City. There was an elevator in the building

Syrup Sandwiches

where my aunt lived on the tenth floor. It was a welcome view compared to that of the train tracks we had. From her window, I could see so many things: other tall buildings, the tree lines of the Eastern hemlocks and tulip trees, and miles of beautiful scenery. It felt so strange to go back to the apartment where my grandmother had once lived. I remember after we got off the elevator on the tenth floor and before my aunt could put the key into the door, my heart sank. I was hoping that I would see my grandmother on the other side of the door. When we went inside, and I saw that my grandmother wasn't there, I struggled to stop myself from crying.

We loved driving to Far Rockaway with Aunt Lillie, and that inspired James and me to learn to use public transportation for our independent adventures. Whenever we wanted to get away from Brooklyn, we would travel by train to boroughs where the population was predominately white. In Queens, Manhattan, and Staten Island, the neighborhoods looked different. The buildings didn't look as rundown as they did at home in Brooklyn. I didn't see many corner stores, and unlike Bushwick, they even had police patrolling the area.

James and I would sometimes get on the train and ride to Manhattan just to see the beautiful tall buildings and watch the many people who seemed to be happier than those of us in Brooklyn. We made sure that we left Manhattan before it got dark because if the police saw us in areas that blacks shouldn't be in, they would arrest us.

We had to learn that lesson the hard way. Once when I was twelve and James was ten, we stayed in Lower East Side Manhattan until it started to get dark. Unfortunately, we had lost track of time, and before we knew it, it was almost eight at night. We were walking back to the train station, and there was a white police officer walking his beat. When he saw us, he called us over to him.

"You boys know you shouldn't be here. I should arrest you," he said.

"Officer, we are going to the train station now. Please don't arrest us," I pleaded.

"Well, then go." The officer pointed down the street toward the train station.

We were both trembling with fear as we headed to the train station. We weren't doing anything wrong, and I couldn't understand why we weren't welcome in that neighborhood. I was sad, not only for me but for James too. I didn't want my little brother to feel like people didn't like him. We were only kids, and the officer said that he should arrest us—just the thought of being arrested and going to jail kept me from sleeping that night. On the train ride home, I told James not to tell our mother about the police incident. If my mother knew what happened, she wouldn't allow us to go back to Manhattan again. Besides, if we told her, it would have just made her angry and sad too. I didn't know if the cop was prejudiced or not. Maybe he was just doing what he was told. Maybe he was just warning us because he knew others who were prejudice and didn't want us to get arrested by one of them. Either way, it still hurt. It still reminded me that life isn't fair.

Chapter 11
Blackout

Summer in the Brooklyn heat felt almost like being in an inferno. The asphalt would get extra hot, and you could see the waves of heat as they formed ripples right before your eyes. When we were lucky enough to have someone who had the right-sized wrench to open the fire hydrants, or "Johnny pumps" as we called them, a heat wave made us happy. One of our neighbors or a random passerby would turn the water on at the Johnny pump. Someone would then take an empty can that had neither top nor bottom and would use the can to funnel water from the Johnny pump toward us. It was a cool, refreshing shower during the sweltering summer days and evenings.

While we were having fun in the water, some cars would stop in the middle of the streaming water so that their cars could get a free wash. We were having fun but not all our neighbors were. When the Johnny pump was turned on, it caused the water pressure in the nearby homes and buildings to become extremely low. So, the tenants would call the police to send someone out to shut the hydrant off. Sometimes we would be outside in the water for hours, and other times it would be less than thirty minutes, depending on whether the tenants wanted to be sympathetic or if the police had more pressing issues to attend to. We knew that the fun was over when we saw the police car arrive. The person holding the water can would normally drop it and haul ass when they saw the police. It was fun playing in the water, but you didn't want to be there when the police arrived. The summers seemed to go by faster when we could play in the hydrants.

In the late summer, my mother would take James and me to buy some of the things that we needed for school. Usually, we went to a thrift store, but I remember one time my mother took James and me to a department store to buy school clothes. It was a hot and steamy day; I was thirteen, and James was eleven.

The department store was owned by a white man. As soon as we walked into the store, he came to the front of the store and asked my mother, "Is there something you need from this store?"

My mother seemed confused as she responded back, "I am here to buy my kids some clothes. Will that be a problem?"

The owner turned around abruptly, mumbled something under his breath, and walked away. As we walked through the store, I saw that the security guard who was initially at the front door when we came in was now following us from aisle to aisle.

I said, "Rena, why does that security guard keep following us?" She flat out said, "Because they think we are going to steal something."

Eventually, the security guard, who was also white came up to my mother and said, "Excuse me. The owner said that you must purchase something or leave the store."

James started to cry because he could not understand why the people in the store were being so mean to us.

My mother said, "Let's go, boys. They don't want our money anyway."

We hadn't been in the store longer than five minutes before we were heading out the door that once greeted us. I had heard from other black kids that they had experienced similar discrimination. Growing up poor and living in the inner city wasn't easy, and when you couple that with racism and discrimination, it eats away at your soul, even as a kid. How do you teach a child not only to understand racism and discrimination but to accept it? James and I needed someone who could explain that to us. We didn't have anyone to sit us down and explain how difficult it was to be discriminated against, how to deal with it, and what to expect. Maybe our fathers could have prepared us to some extent for some of the harsh realities of life. But James and I did the best we could, talking over what happened to us or what we'd observed. We discussed how we could have handled situations better and tried to prepare ourselves for the next encounter.

But we also talked about what we could do to improve our lives. One particularly sweltering evening right after the sun had gone down, James and I sat on the fire escape and watched train after train go by. We talked about being able to apply for the summer job program when we turned fourteen years old and how much fun that would be. James was now eleven and maturing quickly. He had a positive attitude and a million-dollar smile that he flashed often. James was quiet and soft spoken and did more listening than talking. I, on the other hand, was the life of the party and talked too much. As I mentioned, like my mother, I had a large gap in between my top front teeth, and I rarely smiled because of it. I hated that gap. People would ask why I didn't smile like James. I usually didn't answer them, giving them my close-lipped impersonation of a smile.

I would be fourteen the following year, and I couldn't wait to apply to the job program. The objective of the youth job program for inner-city youth was to provide work experience during the summer months to help the youth gain skills for employment. The program provided exposure to the work world and helped develop good work habits such as punctuality, showing up to work regularly, and being able to work well with others. I think another reason why the program was created was to help reduce crime. Most inner-city youth lived in high-crime areas throughout the city. The program gave the youth an opportunity for employment and less time on the street to get into trouble because there was nothing else to do.

As we sat on the fire escape imagining my next summer, James and I heard one of the trains come to a sudden stop. It was a loud grinding noise; it must have been the train's emergency brakes. We quickly jumped up, looked at the stopped train, and then looked down toward the ground and saw a pool of blood and guts. The train had run over someone. We couldn't believe what we saw. The person's insides were all over the street. The smell was so strong and disgusting that we had to hold our noses to keep from getting sick. It was a smell that I will never forget. I thought that the smell of our burning building was terrible, but this smell was far worse. There were pieces of the man's legs, arms, skull, and torso just lying in the street. I think we were both in shock as we just stared at the bloody remains.

Suddenly, we heard the loud sirens of the rescue vehicles. I thought *what a terrible way to die.* I wasn't sure if the man had intentionally jumped in front of the moving train or if he had been pushed. Unfortunately, people being pushed in front of moving trains wasn't an uncommon occurrence. It was in fact, a byproduct of the rise in crime. People being pushed in front of trains was happening throughout New York City during this time. I went to bed that night wondering if the man who died had any children, a mother, or maybe even a wife. It was extremely difficult to fall asleep with the thought of seeing a person's body parts all over the street. I was thinking that his family would miss him and feel sad that he's gone. I never thought about him having a father, as most fathers weren't present, at least not that I was aware of.

Sometimes, when life got rough, we looked to our favorite distraction. James and I loved baseball. I guess you could say we were fanatics. I loved the New York Mets, and James loved the New York Yankees. We thought that they were the best teams in all of baseball. Collecting baseball cards was our passion. I think we had all the baseball cards of both New York teams and many from other teams. I still have them to this day. We would listen to baseball games on a portable radio while we sat on the fire escape. One hot, muggy Wednesday evening (I remember the day: July 13th, 1977), James and I were listening to the New York Mets playing the Chicago Cubs at Shea Stadium in Queens, New York. It was the bottom of the sixth inning and the Mets were losing, 2–1. It was nine thirty at night. Suddenly, the lights went out in the apartment. My first thought was that my mother hadn't paid the electric bill. However, I quickly realized that wasn't the problem because all the streetlights were out too. What was going on? It was a blackout.

We heard a rising swell of yelling and screaming, "Blackout! Blackout!"—so terrifying that we climbed back into our apartment to join our petrified mother. We heard glass breaking, and then the looting started. I looked out the window and could see people pushing grocery carts filled with groceries down the streets. They had clearly broken into the A&P grocery and were taking everything out of the store. I was unhappy that they had vandalized the one place where I spent so much of my time trying to make some money. The police were nowhere to be found.

It seemed that people were breaking into and destroying all the stores along our street, Brooklyn's Broadway Avenue. We saw people carrying household goods from the furniture stores. There were two people carrying what looked like a nine-foot couch down the street, and a lady was carrying a lamp in each of her hands as she ran past the men with the couch. We also saw was a man carrying a television. Then two men approached him, one with a bat and the other with a knife. They snatched the television right out of his hands.

From our portable radio, we learned people were not only looting in Brooklyn but all over New York City. After the looters smashed the windows and stole all they could, they would set the businesses on fire. We watched this happen right from our window in disbelief and fear. As they approached our street, we could see them vandalizing the stores next to our apartment. Finally, they were at our apartment building, which sat atop a pharmacy.

The sounds of breaking glass were loud and now directly beneath the apartment building. The mob had now reached the pharmacy below. The looters carried everything out of the pharmacy that they could move. I saw one man carrying one of those small refrigerators used to store medicines. Another man, smiling like a child, carried an armful of bottled medicines, most of them falling as he ran.

Ultimately, a group of looters set the pharmacy on fire, spurring other looters to run for their lives. We were upstairs looking out the window at our apartment building being set on fire. We were too afraid to leave while the mob was downstairs, but we knew we couldn't stay where we were much longer.

Syrup Sandwiches

Fortunately for us, the mob quickly headed to their next target. Since the fire was directly in our apartment building and not the building next to us, the fire spread quickly. The smoke was heavy and dense and was in our apartment before we knew it. My mother started screaming, "Oh, my God!"

Immediately, I picked up Rhonda and used my shirt to cover her nose to protect her from the smoke. It was difficult to see, and my eyes were tearing. I could hear James and my mother behind us gasping for air as they followed closely. As I ran down the stairs with Rhonda, trying to protect her from the smoke and at the same time wiping my eyes, which were now blurry, I almost lost my footing as I slipped down three steps. I regained my balance but no sooner than I did, someone from another apartment ran into us, causing us to fall. Hysterical and crying, Rhonda landed on me; but since she was in my arms, she wasn't hurt during the fall.

My mother saw us fall and immediately yelled, "Are y'all OK?" I didn't respond. But I guess she had her answer when she saw me stand up with Rhonda in my arms and move on ahead.

As they struggled to get out, neighbors were yelling. They sounded terrified. I heard someone growl over and over, "Get out of my way! Get out of my way!" I saw him push a woman down as he rammed by us.

By the time we made it to the first floor to exit the building, we could barely breathe from the smoke. The heat from the flames was so intense that it felt like we might be burned. I could hear wood crackling. Then suddenly the sounds of the building crumpling behind us and above us was enough to cause everyone to panic. Thankfully, we all made it out safely, but we had a difficult time catching our breath, as our lungs were filled with smoke. We were all coughing, but my mother was in the worst shape, coughing, gasping for air, and crying at the same time. I remember she clutched her pocketbook, the only thing that she had brought with her.

This time the building was more damaged than from the previous fire, and this time we'd made our escape during a blackout. We didn't know what to do. We were in the streets surrounded by looters and people running and destroying everything in sight.

It was dark and we didn't have flashlights, so we relied on the light of the moon to help us walk over to my Aunt Denise's house. This walk was much longer and more dangerous than any other time I remembered. As we were walking and still trying to recover from all the smoke that we inhaled, there were times that we had to run and hide behind parked cars to avoid being trampled by the herds of looters running with stolen goods in their hands. My mother was trying to comfort Rhonda, who was still terrified and crying. She was only five, and I could only imagine how frightening it was for her. Truth of the matter—we were all afraid. My mother led us safely to my aunt's house. I believed she prayed the entire trip that we would be safe there. Although my aunt didn't have lights, her street wasn't a commercial thoroughfare like Broadway Avenue. The brownstone she lived in wasn't likely to be set ablaze.

The blackout lasted for twenty-four hours, and the unimaginable events of hours of looting, arson, and violence were unforgettable. We later found out that the Bushwick section of Brooklyn had sustained the worst damage and destruction of the five boroughs in New York. In all, forty-five stores had been set on fire. A few days after the blackout, there were twenty-three more buildings that were set on fire in Bushwick.

The damage to our building was so severe that we were not allowed to move back into our apartment. The apartments on the second floor had sustained too much damage, and the city deemed the entire building

Syrup Sandwiches

unsafe. The owner of the apartment building would have to get the building up to code and regulation before he could have tenants in the building again. They gave us two weeks to get everything out. We didn't have much: just two beds, two dressers, a couch, a small television, some clothing, and other small stuff.

Rhonda's father, Greg, knew a man who had a small truck. We loaded the furniture and our belongings in the truck and took it to my Aunt Denise's house, where we stayed for almost three months. My mother was placed on the priority apartment relocation list that the city had for families in immediate need. The city found us an apartment in another part of Bushwick on Cornelia Street.

When I started high school in September, I was fourteen. I had just dealt with the blackout, moving, and trying to get settled into a new apartment; and now I didn't have enough clothing for school. There were a tremendous number of thoughts running through my mind. The new apartment building was a beautiful, three-story brownstone. There were three bedrooms, a kitchen, a living room, and a bathroom. It was much bigger than our last apartment on Broadway Avenue and was well maintained. Our new apartment was on the third floor.

There was a fire escape, but it was in the back of the building. The view from the fire escape was nothing like the view on Broadway because we were only able to see the backyards of all our other neighbors. Some of our neighbors had grass in their backyards, while others had concrete. Two of our neighbors had planted vegetables, and we could see the blossoming collard greens and beautiful bell peppers.

It was strange not hearing the passing trains both day and night. I was so used to all the noise that came from the trains, the shoppers on Broadway, and the busy traffic that the silence at our new home was an eerie but welcome change of pace. It was like working in a noisy factory for four years and then suddenly working in a library. Cornelia Street was even a one-way street, so we were able to play street games with fewer interruptions.

Chapter 12
Bullies

My assigned high school was Alexander Hamilton Vocational and Technical, which was named after Alexander Hamilton, a statesman and politician and one of the Founding Fathers of the United States. The school was built in 1903 and had been designed by the well-known New York City school architect, Charles B. J. Snyder.

Hamilton High School was an all-boys school during my first year but would change to allow girls the following year. The school was not your typical high school. We were taught subjects like English, math, and science, but the curriculum included more in-depth instruction than regular schools on various trades such as typewriting, photocopier repair, and cooking.

The school was in the middle of several project buildings named the Albany projects, which were owned and managed by the city and were created to provide more affordable housing for families with low incomes. Albany projects consisted of nine apartment buildings, each of which held more than 130 apartments and were thirteen or fourteen stories tall. Crime was out of control there and would often filter into the school. There were gangs that would frequently rob the teachers as they were exiting the building on their way home. The police would patrol the area near the school, but that didn't deter the criminals.

I was six feet, five inches tall and weighed 192 pounds. I had broad shoulders and looked extremely slim. I was also shy and quiet then, not the talkative life of the party. These attributes made me a high-value target for bullies wanting to look tough. My first year in high school was difficult, as I had to defend myself almost daily from students who tried to intimidate, fight, or steal from me.

I was in class one day, sitting toward the back, when the student sitting in the chair immediately in front of me decided to turn around and snatch the small silver chain that I wore around my neck. This bully belonged to a gang that wreaked havoc outside of the confines of the school. He was shorter than me, probably five feet, five inches, but he weighed more, about 270 pounds. He was stocky like a bulldog. I do not know what I was thinking, but I jumped out of my seat and swung at him with all my strength. I punched him repeatedly. He grabbed me, and we fought, rolling on the floor, and knocking over desks and chairs before anyone could break up the fight.

After the fight, I noticed that I had bloodied his nose. This surprised everyone, including me. When it was time to leave school, I knew that he and his goons would be outside waiting. I was terrified to leave the building, but I had to go home. There was no school security guard back then that I could ask to escort me. I was on my own. As I left the school, I looked around nervously as I made my way to the city bus stop. To my surprise, there was no one outside waiting for me. I was able to make it home safely that day. But, thinking about the fight and wondering what tomorrow might hold, I could not sleep that night.

The next day at school seemed like an ordinary day. I didn't see the bully that I'd fought the day before, and no one said anything to me. Everything was

Syrup Sandwiches

surprisingly calm. However, as I was walking down the hallway going to my next class, two guys tried to jump me. They came from the nearby stairway. I can still see them in my mind. One of them had on a black sweatsuit and wore a blue ball cap. He had a scar on his forehead and was probably five feet, eight inches, and the other one was even shorter, maybe five feet, six inches and wore a pair of blue jeans and glasses. They both looked furious and were repeatedly saying to each other, "Get him."

They both swung at me, trying to hit me as I moved from left to right avoiding as many of their punches as possible. All those days of playing tag had helped with my elusiveness. Suddenly, one of the guys grabbed me and had me on the floor. As he held me down, his partner reached down to assault me. That's when I kicked the first one off me. I wanted to yell for help, but I thought that would make me look weak, so I didn't. Instead, I fought them both for as long as I could. When the hallway started filling with more students, the assailants ran away. I couldn't stay focused in class after the attack. I was glad that the next day would be Friday and the week would finally be over.

Unfortunately, the next day came sooner than I wanted, and I was back in school. I had just finished my first class and was on my way to the next one. As I was walking down the concrete stairs, I saw a guy walking toward me, then he punched me hard in the face. I tumbled down the concrete stairs. That's all I remember. When I came to, my mother was in the ambulance with me, nervous and crying. When I got to the hospital, the doctor gave me ten stitches above my right eye. Before I knew it, I was back home all bandaged up. I lay in the bed with my eye throbbing, wondering if this attack was the beginning of something worse. I was afraid. And my heart raced. I wanted to talk to an adult male because I was not sure what my next move should be. It was in moments like these when I felt lost and the most pain of being neglected. I couldn't imagine having a child and letting him or her go through something like this alone. I would want to be there to hear their feelings and provide some level of support, comfort, and advice.

To my surprise, I never had any more problems from that bully or his cronies. I was glad my prayers were answered. Regrettably, he would not be the last bully that I had to deal with. I believe that one of the things that helped me thwart off the attacks from bullies was that I was fast and could fight well. In fact, I was surprised that I had the natural ability to fight as well as I did. It was never tested until high school, and then I had to fight almost every week.

As bad as my first year of high school was, I did have the pleasure of having Mr. Jankowski as my English teacher. Mr. "J"—that's what I called him—was a middle-aged Jewish man from Haifa, Israel. He had a bald spot and a round face with red chubby cheeks. He wasn't tall, maybe five six, and his slim frame made him look thinner than he probably was. He would tell the class stories about living in Israel and how his country always seemed to be at war. Mr. "J" realized that I enjoyed English and would go out of his way to assign me special projects so that I could get better at writing and composition. I enjoyed going to his class. There was never a dull moment because he made sure that all the students participated in every assignment and that they completed the class projects.

I was one of the tallest kids in school. There were a few members of the school's basketball team who were taller, but they didn't have the problem of being bullied as they had each other for support. Since I was a loner

Syrup Sandwiches

the predatory students thought I'd be an easy target. It seemed as if the bullies at my school believed that if they could intimidate and beat up the tall, quiet guy, then they could earn some bragging rights.

I never had a fight with anyone my height—it was the guys that were a lot shorter than me. Maybe they had a Napoleon complex, but it turned out bad for them when I would kick their asses. Often, students would ask why I beat up on someone who was smaller than I was. I would tell them that I didn't start the fight, I only finished it, and they should have left me alone. They would shake their heads and walk off like they truly didn't understand. But they weren't bullies and didn't get the appeal of a big target.

Because I was tall, most people assumed that I should be playing basketball—the truth was that I loved baseball. I tried out for the school's baseball team and was accepted. I could play any position, but the coach wanted me to play first base. I really wanted to play short stop or the outfield. The coach told me that I was too tall to play short stop. However, I would eventually get to play the outfield.

Then, the coach of the high school basketball team wanted me to play basketball and said, "My team is in need of one more big man to play center. We could use your talents."

I thought about what the coach said about playing basketball even though I knew I probably wasn't good enough. Then it dawned on me that there were more girls at the basketball games, and the players seemed like they were having more fun. For us baseball players, we played baseball outside in the cold at the beginning of the season, and the basketball players always played inside, where it was warm and comfortable. So, I quit the baseball team to join the basketball team. That switch didn't last but one season. As it turned out, I was better at baseball, and all the coach's efforts weren't good enough to turn me into the player he needed me to be.

Now I realize that even though I played both sports, my passion had been baseball; and since my heart hadn't been completely into basketball, I didn't give it my all. To this day, I tell my son, "Always follow your passion, and give it your all."

Chapter 13
Summer Job

It was June and I would turn fifteen years old in August, so I was eligible to apply for the summer job program. It was a real job, not one at the grocery store packing bags for tips but one that paid decent money. New York City's Summer Youth Employment Program (SYEP) provided work experience to economically, disadvantaged youth through jobs during the summer with the objective of helping them to develop skills that might lead to future careers.

To be eligible, you had to be between fourteen and twenty-one years old. I had to provide proof of identity, proof of address, proof of family income, and proof that I was eligible to work. We called these "working papers," and they were provided by the school. The city wanted to verify that potential workers were enrolled in school and attending classes. I was told all the eligibility criteria had to be met before I could apply for the program, and then I had to be selected through a lottery system.

Once I was selected to work, I was excited for the opportunity to work and to be able to help my mother provide for James and Rhonda. The summer job program allowed the workers to work forty hours per week, and I couldn't wait. I knew that I would still pack groceries on the weekends. I had to stay busy and working allowed me to do just that. I was determined to bust my ass working hard. We had bills to pay—the food bills were increasing, and I needed more clothing.

My first summer job was in a section of Brooklyn called Brownsville. When you're accepted into the Summer Youth Program, you don't get a choice as to where in the city you'll be assigned to work. Luckily, my new job was in Brooklyn. But I asked myself, *why Brownsville?* From the 1800s up until the 1950s, most of Brownsville's residents were Jewish. The Jews moved out of the area when the New York Housing Authority started developing public housing. By 1970, Brownsville had an influx of poor minorities. Shortly after these housing projects were built, crime increased, and the poverty prevailed.

There was a string of arsons in the 1970s in New York City that severely devastated the disadvantaged communities. Brownsville was one of the communities that was hit the hardest. Many of the dwelling structures were seriously damaged or destroyed. Now I had a job there, and I was getting nervous, even afraid. Plus, I didn't even know what kind of work I would be doing, and I wouldn't find out until Monday morning. This was Friday, and I was so wired and anxious, I didn't sleep well the entire weekend.

Monday morning, I woke up early and boarded my first of two trains to Brownsville. I had to report to work at eight that morning at a neighborhood community center in Brownsville. It was there where a group of about twenty of us summer workers would learn what our work schedule and assignments would be. I learned that I would be doing custodian assistance work, which meant that I would help clean buildings, office spaces, or warehouses. The custodian team that I was a part of had eight members, including myself. Our first assignment was to clean out a vacant lot. This project hardly fit my impression of a good job, but it didn't matter because I was still motivated by a the thought of getting a real check and looked forward to seeing what my first check would look like.

My official working hours were eight in the morning until five in the evening with an hour for lunch. There was a driver who drove us to our locations for our daily assignments. His name was Mr. Peter, and he had the smallest head I've ever seen. He was a tall black gentleman, about six feet, two inches. He appeared to be in his late forties or early fifties, which was old to me, but then again, I was only fourteen years old; everyone over twenty looked old to me.

Mr. Peter had a one-sided beard. He had hair only on the right side of his face. I couldn't understand how hair would only grow on one side of a person's face. So, being young and inquisitive, I asked. "Why don't you just shave the hair off your face, Mr. Peter?"

"It keeps growing back," he said. That was my cue to leave it alone and not say anything else about his facial hair, and I never did. We would later find out that he had a rare skin condition.

Mr. Peter drove us around in a fifteen-passenger van that had all our required cleaning supplies, including gloves and face masks like the ones we wore during the COVID-19 pandemic. Gloves and masks were required when we would go into buildings that had asbestos, which many of them did. The buildings that didn't have asbestos had fiberglass insulation. It turned out the job was more dangerous than we knew.

The abandoned lot Mr. Peter took us to was once the site of an apartment building demolished many years prior. This lot was filled with rock, glass, sand, and more trash than we wanted to clean. Mr. Peter called someone on the phone to bring us some trash bags, shovels, and rakes. The eight of us cleaned, bagged, and raked at least thirty leaf-sized garbage bags, and this was by eleven in the morning, right before we went to lunch. By the time that I got home that night, I was more tired than I had ever been, so, falling asleep wasn't a problem. When Tuesday morning came, my entire body was sore, and I wasn't moving as fast as I had on Monday morning. I was hoping that when I got to work Tuesday, they would tell me that I was working at a different location and not that abandoned lot. As expected, I wasn't that lucky, and we would be working on that lot for the next two weeks.

I was making the minimum wage of $2.30 an hour. I didn't get paid after working two weeks as I thought I would. I had to work three weeks before my first check. When I got my check, it was $92 before taxes. That seemed like a lot of money to me back then; that's the equivalent of about $405 before taxes today. I was finally making money, and my enthusiasm increased significantly. I started feeling like I had a real purpose; and I believed that if I continued to work hard, it would pay off in the long run. There was no looking back. I was hooked. My job was exhausting, but I had to do it. I felt the support of my family was on my shoulders and couldn't let my family down. My mother, no longer on welfare, was receiving disability, which didn't begin to cover the needs of three children. James earned as much as he could bagging groceries. Rhonda, of course, was too young to work.

I remember lying in the bed, aching from the day's labor, and thinking how different it would be if we had another parent to help support us. It led me to thinking about the father that I had never met and whether I had any brothers or sisters back in Georgia. I wondered if I had any living grandparents and if they knew anything about me. *Had my father ever mentioned me to them?* Too many thoughts at night kept me up. I couldn't find any answers for the many questions that I had. I knew that I was struggling with the reality of not having a father and trying to grow up and be as mature as I could. I wanted somehow to be a good example for my brother and sister.

I worried about my mother because her asthma had gotten worse. She had so much to deal with on top of that, including trying to keep a roof over our heads and keeping us fed and clothed. I believe my mother was unaware that she was motivating me to become more mature and to accept responsibilities. She showed me how not to give up, no matter how dire a situation might be. I saw courage from my mother as she dealt with so many challenges and not knowing if she'd make it through them.

I loved my mother—so many times I didn't tell her that because I assumed that she knew that I loved her. Not knowing how to show my love for her, I just said nothing. I portrayed the image of one who was strong and let nothing ever bother me. In fact, on many nights when my mother was crying herself to sleep, so was I.

After cleaning the abandoned lot for the past six weeks, we finally had an assignment that involved cleaning the inside of a vacant office complex. This was a welcome change. Finally, we were not working outside in the scorching summer heat or the occasional torrential rain. My summer job was getting easier. Maybe I was getting used to working on a regular schedule and it didn't bother me as much anymore. My goal was to work as hard as I could and never be late for work. For me, being on time meant being early. I despised tardiness. I remember one time when Mr. Peter was thirty minutes late picking us up after he dropped us off at a work site. When he showed up, all he said was, "Are you guys ready?" I wanted so badly to say, "Hell, yes, Little Head!" Thank goodness my common sense was working that day.

With my first paycheck, I purchased my first wristwatch, a Timex with automatic dial that displayed the date and day of the week. It had a gold-plated band. The watch wasn't brand-new. I paid two dollars for it, but I still felt like I had achieved something. It was this used watch that had shown me that Mr. Peter was late.

It was interesting how two months of working during the summer could go by so fast. One day when I left work, I was so tired that I had forgotten that we no longer lived on Broadway Avenue. I found myself getting off the train and walking to my old apartment, forgetting that we had moved to Cornelia Street, which was about five blocks away. Just looking at that building and all the difficult and challenging times we had while we lived there would send chills down my spine. I had flashbacks of me and my family running out of that building while it was burning. I could still remember the smell of the heavy smoke as it filled my nostrils, temporarily blinding me as I ran toward the exit, gasping, and coughing as the flames were getting closer and closer. I also remembered the smell of the dismembered man's body after it was run over by the train. Then I thought about all the times that James and I would sit on the fire escape and talk and watch the trains go by or eavesdrop on the conversations of the pedestrians.

It was bittersweet, the bad memories mixed with good memories of James and me on the fire escape. As I headed toward Cornelia Street, I realized that as bad as things had been, there were some good times and dreams of a better life to be thankful for.

Chapter 14
Brownstone

Cornelia Street was a well-deserved blessing. The block was quiet and all the apartments on the street were well kept and without litter or debris scattered all over the place. What I loved more than anything about our new apartment was the fact that there were no roaches or mice ruling our apartment—it was our home, and we didn't have to share it with them. There were only two other families in the building with us, and they kept their apartments clean, so pest control was easier. Without roaches aggravating their asthma, my mother and brother were able to breathe better than they could on Broadway Avenue.

The summer of hard work in Brownsville had come to an end. I had been able to save a little money while working for the last two months and was able to help my mother with groceries. I even bought Rhonda some clothing. But maybe not enough. She was six years old and growing faster than I was getting paid. Now that the summer job was over, it was time to get ready for the school year. I had just turned fifteen and hoped that this year would be better than last year, and that people would leave me alone.

As a sophomore in high school, I started to appreciate being taught things which were once foreign to me like algebra and political science. English was still my favorite subject. I loved that writing allowed me to be as creative as my mind would allow, and I looked forward to writing essays. However, my sophomore year in high school was not much different than my freshman year. I continued fighting more than I wanted as people persisted in trying to bully me. I felt insecure in school whenever a subject came up about my family life or discussions about my father. The teacher once asked everyone in the class to raise their hands if their mother and father both lived in the same house. I wanted to crawl under the table. I just sat there expressionless as half the class raised their hands. The teacher was trying to make the point that single-parent households were common and that there was nothing wrong with families that didn't have two parents.

I remember how emphatically she spoke. "Just because you have two parents in a home, doesn't always mean that you are better off!" I still felt uneasy and empty, not that my mother wasn't doing the best that she could, but that I didn't know who my father was. While I appreciated the fact that she was trying to make us feel better, it did nothing to change my situation. While there was nothing wrong with my family situation, it was certainly difficult to be raised in a family with no father or an abusive father. And on some level, it made things a little worse as it seemed as if that fact was being ignored. I did need a father. James needed a father. All children need a good father.

By sophomore year, I had become even shyer. I even became reluctant to eat in front of passengers on the train. I felt that it was rude to eat in front of others if I was unable to share. I couldn't explain why I felt that way and don't know why I should have even cared. People ate in front of me all the time, and it didn't seem to bother them in the least.

Despite my introversion, I was doing great in school and had solidified my position on the school's baseball team. I was finally able to start in the position of outfielder. I was allowed to play center field. This position allowed me to get most of the outfield plays, so I was not as inactive as the left or the right fielders.

The bullies still felt that they should try their luck at beating up the tall guy. I noticed that most of the students who were bullied just gave in to their oppressors and allowed them to have their way. I couldn't allow myself to be bullied. I had a younger brother who might be in a similar situation, and I wanted him to see that standing up for oneself is essential. I also wanted James to stand strong against abuse, be it physical or emotional, whether it was being done to him or he was in the position to be the abuser. I wanted him to see that there was no place for abuse or bullying. I didn't want James to grow up and be like the men in our lives who showed little compassion or love for anyone and abused at will. I wanted the cycle of abuse to stop in our family, so I had to stand up to the bullies. Sometimes I wondered if the root problem of abusers was that they didn't feel compassion or love for themselves.

The men in my family were bullies to the women in their lives and showed no regard or concern that what they were doing had a negative impact emotionally, not only for their intended victims but also on children like myself, James, and our cousins. By being forced to witness their abuse, we were ultimately subjugated to the same emotional abuse as the victims. We, too, were abused, just on another level.

The good thing about living on Cornelia Street in the brownstone meant that I could go outside anytime and sit on the front stoop. The stoop replaced the fire escape that James and I were used to. The peacefulness of my new neighborhood took some getting used to. There were no people walking past the apartment yelling or arguing, no loud trains, and no loud car horns, no loud traffic interrupting my thought process. I was free to daydream at will.

Even though we were no longer living on Broadway Avenue and dealing with the issues we dealt with there, we now had to deal with a neighborhood gang that would chase James and me as we walked from the train station or throughout the neighborhood. They called themselves the Savoir Faire Gang. *Savoir faire* is a French term that means being adaptable and knowing what to do in any situation. How in the hell did a neighborhood street gang come up with a French name? It was like these thugs decided to become just educated and creative enough to come up with a name that would make them look like they were smart while they were robbing or beating you up.

At the time, we didn't know what *savoir faire* meant, and we had to look it up in the encyclopedia at the library just to see who the hell was chasing us. It's pretty sad that the gang was smart enough to have a unique name but not smart enough to know that stealing and assaulting people was illegal. The gang only had about eight members, and they were between the ages of thirteen and eighteen. We were fortunate that they were never fast enough to catch James or me but not for lack of trying. They would often pop up out of nowhere as we were going to the store, or from the train stop, and ultimately back to our apartment.

One day the Savoir Faire Gang finally had James and me surrounded. There were six of them at the time, elated and all smiles for catching us yet angry that it had taken them so long. As the circle of gang members surrounding us closed in, punches started flying. James and I swung back on the crew with all the energy and might that we could muster, repeatedly swinging and throwing punch after punch. This went on for what seemed like twenty minutes. Before the gang could expend their total fury upon us, we were able to find an opening in the circle of misfits and quickly escape. They chased us for about three blocks before they gave up, angry and dejected. That must have been the fastest that I ever ran. I don't know what happened to the gang. They just fizzled out. They probably got arrested or beat up by a real gang.

    We never told our mother about the gang. The last thing that we wanted was to give her something else to worry about. Like other times I faced trouble, I wished I could have had a man in my life to talk to. I realized the importance of being there as a father when things get rough for your sons—especially when they're teenagers. James and I would have appreciated knowing a kind and sensible man that we could have shared our experiences with and gotten advice from.

Chapter 15
Gainfully Employed

In July, I was happy to be selected by the Summer Youth Employment Program for the second year in a row. I would turn sixteen the following month. Once again, my work assignment landed me in Brownsville cleaning out vacant lots and abandoned buildings.

This year, Mr. Peter wasn't our driver. We had a short, Hispanic man with a thick mustache named Mr. Rivera. There was never a dull moment with Mr. Rivera. He drove the van excessively fast like he was racing another vehicle. However, we would be on a one-lane street going in one direction. Some of the workers would gasp as Mr. Rivera would turn from one block to the next. One day, he turned the corner so fast that a few of the workers became unseated and found themselves on the floor looking up. I was prepared for Speedy Gonzalez and knew that had I not held on tightly, I, too, would be spread out like an area rug.

We asked Mr. Rivera if he could please slow down, but he would say, "No speak English." I knew he was lying because I heard him on the phone one day giving someone directions to his house, and it was all in English. He only acted as if he couldn't speak English when he didn't want to be bothered.

I reported him to the people who were in charge at the office where we worked, and they said that they would take care of it. I am not sure if they really had a thorough conversation with Mr. NASCAR, but a few

Syrup Sandwiches

days later he was only driving fifteen miles over the speed limit. I left it alone. At least I felt like he wouldn't kill us at that speed.

Once again, the summer went by too fast, and it was time to go back to school. I was a junior in high school and had just turned sixteen. I was excited because I could finally apply for a job that wasn't seasonal. Some people were excited about turning sixteen because they'd have a big party with all their friends and would probably get a bunch of gifts, maybe even their first car. But James and I never had a real birthday party with ice cream, cake, balloons, and gifts. Our mother couldn't afford it.

When James turned seven and I turned nine, we did have an ice cream cake from Carvel. I remember my mother walking into the room with the cake behind her back, and as soon as she walked into the apartment, she said, "Surprise! Happy birthday, boys!"

At sixteen, having a party was the last thing on my mind. I was happy and excited to be able to work more hours. That was my birthday gift.

I applied for a job at McDonald's, and they hired me. After three weeks of training, I was allowed to work the grill. The work wasn't hard, but it did become boring to repeatedly turn burgers on a hot grill for five hours. After school, I would rush over to McDonald's to start my shift and would work until nine at night. On the weekends, I was able to put in more hours and would work overtime if they needed me. Working the summer jobs taught me the importance of being punctual and the value of being dependable. I carried these qualities over to McDonald's. I made sure that I learned everything about the restaurant, including the various positions, the food ordering and stocking processes, and creating the employee weekly schedules. I would often ask to work different positions. I was determined to give the job at the restaurant my best effort. As a result, it didn't take management long to realize that I was reliable and a hard worker. Within six months, they offered me the position of Crew Chief.

The restaurant had an owner, three managers, and two crew chiefs, including me. As a crew chief, I had to be proficient at all positions in the restaurant. I was responsible for ensuring that all the employees knew how to work their respective positions and I had to know how to provide assistance when needed.

The restaurant was in a section of Bushwick known as Ridgewood. The area wasn't safe, especially at night, and the restaurant had been robbed twice in the last eight months. I never witnessed any robberies at the store, but Brenda, one of the store's managers, told me that she was there during one of the robberies.

She said, "It was thirty minutes before closing. Back then the restaurant closed at eleven at night. Two guys came into the restaurant with masks on and they both had guns. They told everyone to get on the floor, except me, and they forced me to open the safe in the back office. Then they ran out of the restaurant as quickly as they ran in and jumped into a car and sped off."

I thought about what Brenda had said and wondered what I would do if faced with the same situation. Would I be as calm as she was, or would I freak out and get myself shot? I didn't want to think about it anymore. I was stressing myself out, and I needed to be calm, cool, and relaxed for my crew.

Working more hours at the restaurant meant that I was making more money and was able to buy more groceries for the family. My mother was proud of me for working so hard and would often say so. But I would downplay it as if it was no big deal and say, "Working hard isn't bad." I was doing what needed to be done, and I hoped that next year James would be able to work so that he, too, could help the family out. I wanted James to experience the same feeling of success that came from working hard and helping to provide for your family. Even at that young age, I knew that would go a long way in helping to end the cycle of neglect caused by men who did not provide for their families. That was my goal and I wanted that for James' future family, too.

During the summer before my senior year, I was stoked. All I could think about was that I would finally be a senior and this would be my last year in school. I hadn't given much thought to what I wanted to do when I graduated. I was thinking about going to a community college or possibly joining the military like my two male cousins, Kem and Bobby. Bobby was the only child of my aunt Odessa. I knew that if I did join the military, it wouldn't be the Army. Everyone that I knew who had joined the military went into the Army. I wanted to be different.

The following year, James was accepted into the summer job program, and he was elated. I remember when he found out that he would be working, he ran through the apartment like he was being chased by the Savoir Faire Gang, shouting, "I have a job! I have a job!" His celebration was short-lived, as our mother yelled out from the other room, "Boy, shut up that noise!"

James attended Bushwick High School. Even though Alexander Hamilton High School was a school with a ton of disciplinary issues and was in a gang-infested neighborhood, Bushwick High School made Alexander Hamilton High School look like a private school. It wasn't uncommon to hear about shootings, robberies, or rapes near the school. Going to Bushwick was like going to school with a sign around your neck that said, "Please assault or rob me today."

James told me that he, too, had to fight while in school, but it was rare. James was a lot shorter than I was. At five feet, seven inches, he didn't attract the attention of bullies or boys trying to make a name for themselves. James was quiet and got along well with almost anyone. He had an infectious smile that was difficult not to reciprocate. The truth was James and I looked nothing alike, even though we had the same mother. Apparently, we got our looks from our fathers, whom neither of us had ever seen.

One day while in school, one of my classmates asked me if I was tall like my father. Not wanting to reveal that I knew nothing about my father, including his height, I said, "I will be taller than him."

Secretly, I was hoping that my classmate would not realize that I didn't answer his question. It obviously worked because he said, "I want to be taller than my father, too."

It was times like these when people asked about my father that I wanted to run and hide. I felt bad that I didn't have a father I knew, and I didn't have a great explanation why. James and I didn't even have the satisfaction of telling people that our fathers and mother didn't get along well or that they both agreed to go their separate ways, which was the case with many of the other children that we knew.

Oftentimes, I would play back in my mind my mother telling me that when she left Georgia, she didn't tell James' or my father that she was going to New York to live. I couldn't help but wonder why neither of our fathers tried to look for us. I'm quite sure that they could have asked around and eventually discovered where Rena had gone.

In the end, it didn't really matter why; it did not change our situation. Somehow, James and I had figured out what we needed and managed to survive in spite of the fact that we didn't know our fathers. We were getting older, and I was becoming my own man. I started saving a little money and was looking forward to moving out of my mother's apartment at some point soon. I wanted her to feel she had one less person who needed her. She had James and Rhonda to parent, guide, and protect. That was enough.

Chapter 16
Career Day

It was November when my school held its annual Career Day, which lasted for three days, go figure! Career Day was customary in the months leading up to graduation in June. Our High School Career Day was a gathering of employers from various organizations, this included all branches of the military that met at the school to talk to the students about their future employment plans and possible careers.

I started my career search walking past the tables that were set up for the military. There were flyers on every table that explained the benefits of joining, and recruiters were animatedly telling kids why their branch of service was a better choice than the others. As I passed the Navy table, one of the recruiters looked directly at me and said, "Son, join the Navy, you will always have three hots and a cot." I thought, *what in the hell is he talking about?* Listening to him further, I found out that he meant three hot meals a day and somewhere to sleep. That was helpful to know and sounded good to me.

The Army was a non-starter because I associated it with being in the woods. Growing up in Brooklyn hadn't prepared me for that. Besides, I was a lot more afraid of the animals that were in the woods than the criminals that passed me on the streets. I knew what to expect from criminals, but not with animals, especially bears. I would only have two chances against them: slim and none. I thought the Marines would be too strict for me, and I knew that I wasn't disciplined enough to join. I also didn't think I had the dedication that it required. The Air Force seemed like a country club for rich people. I thought that all they did was fly planes and they never had to get their hands dirty. The Coast Guard was just like the Navy to me, and I really didn't know the difference between the two except that the Navy had bigger ships.

I had every intention of going to a community college in Queens. I thought studying electronics or computers would be good. On the last day of the Career Day, the Navy recruiter was somehow able to get me to commit to his coming by the house and telling me more about the Navy. For about two months, I avoided him. Finally, I allowed him to come to the apartment to tell me all about the Navy. At least it would get him off my back. Once again, I thought that having a father or a close male that I could talk to about decisions that I might make would have made the process less stressful for me. Every time I needed someone to talk to and didn't have anyone just made me that more determined to ensure that I never allowed that to happen to any child of mine. When I was making critical decisions about my future, it was a terrible and lonely feeling not to have any male support.

The recruiter went through his normal spiel of trying to inform me about the Navy and all that it had to offer. He recited the reasons why I would be good for the Navy and how I could build a career and earn a living while attending college classes. Next, he asked me what seemed like a thousand questions about my life. He wanted to know whether I had ever been arrested or convicted of a crime. Did I do drugs? Did I have any children? And many more questions. After about two hours, this interrogation in my mother's kitchen ended.

The recruiter informed me that he could set up an appointment to take the Armed Services Vocational Aptitude Battery (ASVAB) at the Military Entrance Processing Stations (MEPS) at Fort Hamilton in Brooklyn. I agreed to take the exam.

The recruiter was a white man, I'd say in his mid-thirties. He had a thick mustache and a stern look on his face. His hair was blond and cut short. When he spoke, he did so with conviction, which made him appear believable. I was only going on my instincts and didn't know if what he was telling me was true or if he was just a salesman for the Navy. But ultimately, I trusted what he was telling me about the Navy and felt that I would give the Navy a chance.

The ASVAB is a timed aptitude test of the United States Department of Defense designed to evaluate a military candidate's abilities in the following areas: arithmetic reasoning, mathematics knowledge, auto and shop information, word knowledge, general science, mechanical comprehension, paragraph comprehension, and electronics information. Administered at Military Entrance Processing Stations (MEPS) and schools nationwide, the ASVAB is an important test to assess which branches of the service you might qualify for and which skills or jobs you might be most suited for. Every branch of service had a minimum ASVAB score that they would accept before they would allow the candidate to join their branch. At the time, the Coast Guard, which was followed by the Air Force, required the highest ASVAB scores. Next was the Navy, followed by the Marines and the Army. If you scored high on the ASVAB, you could pick any branch of service that you wanted to serve in.

Three weeks later, I arrived at the Fort Hamilton Army Base in Brooklyn to take my ASVAB. That was my first time visiting a military base, and I was amazed

Syrup Sandwiches

at all the landmarks. The base had more trees than I'd ever seen. The view was magnificent, as it overlooked the Verrazano-Narrows Bridge and parts of the Atlantic Ocean. Although Fort Hamilton was an Army base, it was also comprised of active-duty Navy, Air Force, Marines, Coast Guard, National Guard, and Reserve components. Fort Hamilton is only five miles from Coney Island, New York City's famous amusement park. The Military Entrance Processing Station (MEPS) at Fort Hamilton evaluates applicants to determine their physical qualifications, aptitudes, and moral standards.

As I sat in what looked like a classroom along with fifteen other test takers waiting for the proctor, I was thinking that it still wasn't too late to get up and leave. But I stayed and took the test. The test was scheduled for three hours. It was grueling for me because they asked questions about subjects that I had no clue about such as automotive engines and equipment related to rural farm life. There was nothing on the exam about the city life that I was accustomed to. When the three hours were up, I just wanted to go home and relax my brain.

The results came back while I was still at the MEPS. I was informed that I had passed the test and that my choices were the Army, Navy, and Marines.

I chose the Navy. I didn't score high enough to be accepted into the Coast Guard or Air Force. I didn't do well in the auto and machinery and the mechanical comprehension categories, primarily due to the lack of exposure in those areas. After taking and passing the test, I was given a physical. There were five people who didn't score high enough on the test to qualify for any branch of service. They all left after getting their results. The physicals were thorough. They checked every part of my body, including hearing and vision.

After passing all my physicals and signing all the required paperwork, I thought that I would finally be allowed to go home. It had been a long day with the lengthy ASVAB test and all the medical exams and paperwork. I was exhausted and had been at the MEPS for eight hours. My bed was calling me.

However, before going home, I also met with my recruiter to determine what would be my best career path. The recruiter told me about all the different career paths that were available to me in the Navy. He said I didn't have to decide what job I wanted to do right away. I was told that I could join first and go in as undesignated. Then, once I was in the Navy, I could try out the various positions and decide which job I wanted to have as a career. I thought that sounded interesting and it gave me the opportunity to explore my options. I was excited about trying out different jobs to figure out the one that I liked most. I was undecided and not sure what I really wanted to do in the Navy. What I did know was that I wanted it to be technical. Finally, after meeting with the recruiter, I was free to go home.

This was my first of the two trips I would have to make to the MEPS. On my next trip back, I would take the Oath of Enlistment and head out to basic training. From that moment, I would become an active member of the U.S. military. As I was leaving Fort Hamilton, I was exhausted, nervous, and uncertain. My uncertainty came from not knowing if my choice to join the military was the right one. Would I be able to adjust to being in the military? At the same time, I was excited because all of this was new to me and the biggest decision of my life. I wasn't due to graduate until the following June. I'd signed up for the Navy under the Delayed Entry Program, which meant that I could join the Navy after passing the ASVAB and physicals and could go to boot camp on an agreed upon later date. That date was June

Syrup Sandwiches

28 of the next year. After I signed up for the Navy's Delayed Entry Program, I attended a Sunday church service to ask God if I had made the right decision to join the military. I didn't get a clear answer to my question, or I wasn't listening hard enough to hear it. Either way, I was still joining the military.

Around the time of my recruitment, I noticed that my mother had stopped going to church as much as she used to. I think that she had gotten tired of the Lord not working in her life the way that she thought He should. My mother didn't seem happy with her life. To me, it seemed that she was missing something and couldn't figure out what it was.

She would often say, "I need a change in my life." When I asked her what kind of change, she would say, "Something better than *this*!" and would point her right index finger and move it from side to side as if she was pointing to everything in the room. She would never say what "this" was. I think my mother was depressed and didn't have an outlet. She had a child about to graduate high school and head to the military and another son who would be turning sixteen in August who was out a lot, working just as hard as I was. Then, again, she also had a daughter who was nine and who still relied heavily on her for everything.

My mother wasn't dating anyone, including Greg. His abuse had finally stopped. As James and I got older, taller, and stronger, Greg was wise enough not to attack our mother again. But all the emotional and physical damage had been done, and my mother was mentally exhausted by the time she finally got rid of Greg.

I remember she said, "Anthony, I am so glad to be done with him." When she said "him," she closed her eyes as if she was trying to erase all the bad memories that he caused her over the years.

    I think she was extremely lonely but would never say it. The church had been her refuge. She spent so many hours of her life there that I think she became burned out. There were times when I would look at my mother's face and see nothing but despair, loneliness, and heartache. I was still a teenager and didn't fully know how or what to say to my mother that would provide the level of comfort that she needed. I tried anyway. One time I told my mother that things would get better, and that God wouldn't put more on her than she could bear. She smiled and gave me a big hug. My mother couldn't hide her emotions well. However, she was a quiet person who kept her deepest thoughts and stories to herself. She didn't share much with James and me. It was almost as if she was protecting us from all that she could have shared.

    By my senior year in high school, I was attending church less often too but still showed up now and again. One Sunday I was glad I had. While listening to the sermon, I saw a young lady a few pews away from me. Her skin was chocolate and she looked like a goddess. Her hair was slightly curly and done well. When she stood up, I saw she was wearing a dress that showed a figure worth noticing. She looked to be about five feet seven. She was slim but not skinny, maybe 130 pounds. She caught my eye. I tried to be discreet, but that didn't work. I was busted, staring at her when I should have been listening to the pastor.

    The pastor was preaching about robbing God. Again. I'd already heard that sermon more times than I needed. *Missing this sermon won't keep me out of heaven,* I thought. After the church service, we normally had a meet-and-greet in the back of the church, so I stuck

Syrup Sandwiches

around to see if I could see up close that woman who had caught my attention. Then there she was—two feet in front of me. I introduced myself first, and she told me her name was Wendy.

"The service was good today, wasn't it, Wendy?" I asked.

I was trying to act as if I was all into the sermon even though I wasn't. She said, "It was OK, but I've heard it too many times." I burst out laughing because I was thinking the same thing earlier. It was hard for me to contain my excitement. Here was someone who felt the same way as did I about this preacher frequently talking about money and tithes. We exchanged numbers and went our separate ways. I thought about Wendy all night and all day for the next few weeks. I had never had a girlfriend or even dated. Maybe that was why I was able to stay focused on my schooling. Needless to say, Wendy stayed on my mind.

After a few weeks of contemplating when I should ask Wendy out, I finally got up the courage to call. I asked her to go out on a date and she said yes. I was thrilled, to say the least. We visited Coney Island Amusement Park on our first date. I was nervous and excited at the same time. After all, I had never done this before. We would go on a few more dates before she became my first girlfriend.

Chapter 17
Sweet Goodbyes

June 1981 was bittersweet, bitter because I would be leaving my family to join the Navy. I thought about leaving my mother to look after James and Rhonda without my assistance and how hard it might be for her. It didn't dawn on me that my mother was caring for all of us, no matter how much I was contributing. I couldn't see that in some ways my leaving might lessen her burden. I would also be leaving Wendy, the first girlfriend that I had ever had. It was strange and exciting caring for a woman that was not my mother or my aunt. The one positive I thought of was by joining the Navy, I wouldn't have to worry anymore about people trying to bully me or being chased by a gang.

My goal was to go into the Navy and learn everything that I could, advance up the ranks, and make as much money as possible. I wanted to ensure that my mother didn't have to go without anything that she wanted ever again. On the back burner, once I got out in the world, I wanted to find my father. I wanted to know if I had any half-brothers and half-sisters or any living grandparents. I kept mulling over these same questions without any answers.

I was seventeen years old and on my way to Fort Hamilton MEPS to be bused to the airport. From there, I would fly out to attend basic training. I was informed that I would be going to Recruit Training Command, we called it boot camp, in Great Lakes, Illinois. At the

Syrup Sandwiches

MEPS, I joined everyone else who was going to basic training and was sworn in by taking an oath.

When taking the Oath of Enlistment, I had to state my name and repeat the following: "I, _____, do solemnly swear (or affirm) that I will support and defend the Constitution of the United States against all enemies, foreign and domestic; that I will bear true faith and allegiance to the same; and that I will obey the orders of the President of the United States and the orders of the officers appointed over me, according to regulations and the Uniform Code of Military Justice. So, help me God" (Title 10 U.S. Code, Armed Forces, Section 502). After the Oath, I was officially in the Navy.

After taking the Oath, we were led from the MEPS to a bus that was waiting to take us to the airport. There were seven of us on the bus, and we all looked nervous on our way to Kennedy Airport. Brooklyn was all that I knew. I had not been outside of New York since I arrived as a two-year-old, and I had never flown. I was anxious about my first flight and didn't know what to expect. I knew that flying was expensive, and I was amazed that all the people in the airport had so much money that they could afford to fly. Fortunately, I didn't have to pay for my flight to Chicago. Traveling throughout the airport was unbelievable. There were people everywhere. Not that I wasn't used to being around a lot of people, especially in Manhattan near 42nd street.

After boarding the plane and taking off, we were in the air for about twenty minutes. The flight was going great. It was smooth and almost felt like we weren't 35,000 feet in the sky. Then suddenly, the plane began to bounce up and down, and I heard some of the passengers scream. I heard the captain's voice on the loudspeaker. He asked that everyone return to their seats. He informed us that the weather had turned bad and heavy turbulence would probably remain throughout the flight. He wasn't wrong. The plane descended, pitched, and rolled so often that I started to get dizzy. This wasn't my idea of what it was like to fly. Would I ever have the nerve to fly again? I sat in my seat, strapped in, and scared as hell, wondering if I would make it to Chicago alive. There were other passengers who were acting as if they weren't on the same plane that I was. They were calm and relaxed; some were even sleeping. Others were smiling as if they enjoyed watching other people who were obviously scared out of their minds.

I had to tell myself, *Stop being a punk. You've been through worse shit than this.* I kept repeating that to myself. It worked for a little while. Then the captain's voice came over the loudspeaker again. He said, "Due to the severe weather, we are in a holding pattern and will be unable to land now. We will continue to circle the airport until the weather is better and we're cleared to land." I think we stayed in the air an additional forty minutes before we could land. This had to be a bad flight even for the frequent fliers.

We finally landed safely at O'Hare International Airport. When I was ready to leave the plane, we went into the terminal and waited. Soon it was time to board a shuttle bus. The automatic doors opened and I was exposed to the most intense heat that I'd ever felt. New York got hot during the summer months, but this Illinois heat was like what I imagined hell might feel like. It was nighttime, and I could not imagine what the heat would feel like during the middle of the day.

We boarded the shuttle bus and were on our way to the Recruit Training Command (RTC) Great Lakes. My first week at boot camp was the in-processing, where they gave me Navy-issued clothing, showed me how to fold and stow them, and showed me how to make my bed—I mean, *bunk*. They gave me another dental and

Syrup Sandwiches

medical exam and shaved my hair even though my hair was already short. The week would be filled with marching, conditioning, attending Navy classes, drilling, and swimming. I had never swam a day in my life.

Boot camp was like I'd imagined and seen on television, but it didn't become real for me until they took me to the swimming pool, had me climb the ladder of a diving board, and told my ass to jump into this Olympic-sized pool. The pool looked to be a hundred feet deep. The excitement of joining the Navy, being able to start a career, and to travel the world had robbed me of my common sense! How did I not realize that knowing how to swim was something that all people in the Navy had to know? I stood on the diving board, knees shaking like I was outside naked in the freezing rain. I feared that I would drown.

I was wondering if they knew that I couldn't swim. No one up until this point had ever asked if I knew how to swim. Most black and brown kids who live in major cities lack access to swimming pools and lessons. I can only assume that they thought that I could swim or else I wouldn't have considered joining the Navy. They were wrong. I jumped off the board and into the water's abyss, kicking and flapping my arms like a bird; and the more that I tried to swim, the deeper I sank. Thankfully, two divers were in the water and came immediately to my rescue. It was then that they knew what I'd known all along: I couldn't swim to save my life! I was assigned to remedial swimming classes for the next two weeks. I had to qualify as a *third-class swimmer:* That was a sailor who could stay afloat and survive in a man-overboard situation without the use of a personal flotation device long enough to be rescued.

As it turned out, swimming was my toughest challenge during boot camp—not the getting up at the crack of dawn, or the marching in the heat of summer, or the rigorous exercise regimes. However, once I was able to successfully float on my back and paddle the length of the pool, I was able to pass the swimming class. Had I failed remedial swimming, I would have been on my way back to Brooklyn.

The seven weeks of boot camp didn't go by fast enough. I kept wondering where my first duty station would be, which job would I be assigned, what would the other sailors be like. Would I be stationed on the East Coast or the West Coast? I wanted to stay on the East Coast to be closer to my family in Brooklyn, but I guessed that was not the Navy's top priority.

No one knows their duty station until boot camp is completed. Once I graduated from boot camp, I was fortunate to get an assignment on the East Coast as I'd hoped. I would be stationed on a supply ship located in Norfolk, Virginia. I reported to the naval ship, the U.S.S. Sylvania. I was an eighteen-year-old straight out of boot camp and ready to see the world. I'd never been on a boat or ship, and to see this large vessel was unbelievable. Since I'd not already selected my career path and wanted to try out the different jobs that were available, I was considered undesignated. Unbeknownst to me, this was not a good thing as all undesignated sailors immediately go to the Deck Department of a ship.

My recruiter knew that and didn't share that essential information with me. Deck Department on a ship is where the Boatswain's Mate (BM) works. The BM trains, directs, and supervises personnel in the ship's maintenance duties. This includes all activities related to ship line handling, boat seamanship, painting, upkeep of the ship's external structure, rigging, deck equipment, decks, seamanship tasks, maintaining equipment used in loading and unloading cargo, ammunition, fuel, and general stores.

Syrup Sandwiches

I hadn't been in the Navy six months, and I was already about to get into trouble. Shortly after reporting to my first ship and being assigned to the Deck Department, the supervisor of the department told me that I had to put on a safety harness and chip the old paint and rust off the side of the ship while inside of a safety net suspended thirty feet above the water. My first thought was he must be crazy. I was already upset with my recruiter that I was in Deck Department and not doing something technical like I wanted. Then for this guy to tell me to chip the ship while hanging over the water was beyond reason. Remember, I can barely swim!

"Hell, no. I'm not doing that!" I told him.

The supervisor immediately stepped in front of me, and he and I almost started fighting before some other shipmates came in between us to break it up. I was sent to the Department Head and was disciplined. I was told that I had to do as I was told, or I would be in more trouble, and it would affect my career. This was not my idea of a career that I wanted. However, since I was undesignated, I didn't have a choice and had to stay in Deck Department for at least six months before I was able to even request a change to a different profession. Changing professions, or "rates" as they were called in the Navy, was not automatic. You had to qualify for a specific position and be accepted.

I thought about my recruiter and wanted to kick his ass the entire time that I was an undesignated. I eventually applied for the career path of Radioman (RM) and was allowed to transfer into that position. As a Radioman (RM), I was responsible for transmitting and receiving radio signals and processing all forms of telecommunications through different avenues of media whether it was onboard ships, shore commands, or aircraft.

Chapter 18
Navy Life

A year after reporting to my first duty station, we were deployed to the Mediterranean Sea for six months. I thought that going out to sea on a ship would be fun. Boy was I wrong. During our transit to the Mediterranean Sea, we met with severe weather. The sea level rise was at twenty-seven feet. The ocean tossed the large vessel around like a toy boat in a bathtub with running water. I wasn't used to sailing and instantly became sick, my equilibrium gone. It was nearly impossible to stand as the ocean had its way with the ship. We all held onto anything that was nailed down. We were in the storm for two days, and I was sick the entire time. That was the worst feeling in my life. I couldn't eat anything because I kept vomiting, and I wasn't the only one sick on the ship. But there were many on the ship who didn't have any problems and had what are known as *sea legs*. Sea legs is the ability of a person to maintain their balance and not become sick when on a moving ship or boat. Later, I would develop sea legs myself, but this first deployment had me wondering over and over again, what was I thinking when I enlisted!

The trip to the Mediterranean Sea took two weeks. Sleeping aboard the ship was a major problem for me. The berthing spaces were small, and I was longer than the racks (beds) that we slept in. Each rack had its own rack light. Sailors used the rack lights for reading and for writing letters back home; but my rack light had

Syrup Sandwiches

to be moved to a different location so that I had enough room to lie in my rack more comfortably. I always slept on the top rack; the bottom and middle racks were out of the question as neither provided enough headroom for me.

Shipboard life in general was difficult. Unless we were visiting a port, we worked extremely long hours, seven days a week. I was a junior sailor, and there were various mandatory responsibilities related to my job and to protecting myself, my shipmates, and the ship during an attack.

During the deployment, we visited France, Italy, Turkey, and Spain. It was amazing to see cultures outside of the United States, but I was happy for our return to Norfolk, Virginia. I had grown tired of the long hours. Although port visits were a diversion, as a junior sailor, I wasn't allowed to stay off the ship for extended periods of time to fully enjoy my port visits. When we pulled back into our homeport, I lived onboard the ship. I did not have the seniority to qualify for a housing allowance to get an apartment off the ship.

After my first deployment, I enrolled in driving school so that I could learn how to drive and then buy a car. I was excited about learning to drive and was able to learn quickly. Within six months, I had a license and owned a gray 1977 four-door Pontiac Bonneville. To finally own a car that, up until now, I could only dream about felt surreal.

When I purchased my vehicle, I was so excited that I called James to share the good news. "James, guess who has a car?" I asked.

"No, you don't!"

"Yes, I do, and it's beautiful."

"Congrats," he said. "Will you teach me how to drive?"

"Of course, I will." James was seventeen and, like me at that age, had never driven a car. He was now more eager than ever to drive.

In May, I was called into the office of my department head and was informed that my mother had contacted the ship to report that my grandfather, Oscar, had passed away. My heart skipped a beat, not because of news about my grandfather but because of the stress and sadness that I imagined my mother must be going through.

After speaking with the department head and receiving his condolences, I requested that I be allowed to return to Brooklyn to attend my grandfather's funeral. I was granted permission to take leave. It was great that we were in our homeport of Norfolk, Virginia, and not on deployment. During our last deployment to the Mediterranean, there was a shipmate whose sister had passed away. Because we were out to sea, getting him off the ship and to a location where he would be able to catch a commercial flight back home took longer than expected, and the sailor wasn't able to make it back in time for the funeral.

Being away from your family is difficult while on deployment, not only for the family members left behind but also for the sailor. The sailor must deal with not being home at times when the family needs them the most, especially during difficult times like the death of a loved one or natural disasters. Being deployed might also mean missing the birth of your child, which is an already emotional and stressful time for the mother and the sailor. Returning home early from deployment for the birth of a child rarely happens unless the mother's or child's life is in danger. I wasn't married during the deployment, so to see how some of the married sailors struggled with missing their spouses or children was eye-opening. Some would cry in their racks or become sad

Syrup Sandwiches

and depressed. It was a tough time for them. I wondered if I were married or had a child how I would handle missing my family: Would I be depressed or sad? Would I break down and cry?

I called my mother back, and she picked up after five rings. She was crying as she was telling me what I already knew, that her father had passed away. It was difficult to hear her so sad and sobbing. She said, "Anthony, my father is dead!"

It was something about the way she said "dead" that instantly made me feel worse.

"He died from a stroke," she said. "Oscar wasn't a good father, but I still loved him, and this hurts so much."

I thought to myself how terrible he was to her, her siblings, and her mother. Then I had an epiphany. I realized this must be what *unconditional love* means.

"Everything will be OK," I assured her. "I'll drive up to Brooklyn and be with you tomorrow."

"OK, Anthony." She sounded slightly relieved.

During my six-hour drive, I had time to reflect and think about my mother's life and how her not having her father in her life the way that she needed probably had a lot to do with the life choices that she made. The void of not being embraced emotionally by her father was never filled. I then returned to brooding about how James and I grew up without a father or any male guidance and the impact that it had on some of the decisions that we made. As I matured fatherless, I went from wanting and needing a father to thinking that it would be OK to feel that it didn't matter anymore. I realized that I couldn't miss something that I'd never had.

I wasn't interested in going to my grandfather's funeral. I lacked any feelings toward him one way or the other because of the way that he'd abandoned his children and continued to treat my mother as less than a daughter. I still found it difficult to understand how my grandfather couldn't embrace my mother and give her the love that she so desperately needed. I don't think that the love from a father for his child should be negotiable. It was tough for me to have any level of respect for my grandfather because of who he was as a person. I was only going to his funeral out of respect for my mother and to be there to support her.

I arrived at my mother's apartment Wednesday, and the funeral was the following Saturday. My mother was a mess, and I could tell that she had shed many tears because her eyes were puffy and red. She was clearly despairing. When my mother saw me, she gave me a big hug and wept on my shoulders. The sight of seeing my mother hurt and emotionally shattered made it difficult for me not to cry the tears that she no longer had. I was happy to see my brother and sister and gave them both a big hug.

Unlike me, James liked our grandfather. I saw early on how he neglected our mother, and James was shielded from a lot of that. He wasn't completely aware of Oscar's shortcomings. Because I didn't have a great relationship with my grandfather, I wasn't particularly upset about going to see him laid out in a casket.

James had just turned eighteen and, unlike me, decided not to join the military. He chose to stay behind and attend college. My sister was twelve and had become a pain in the ass for my mother, nagging her for money to buy candy or anything else that wasn't good for her. Rhonda was older now and looked more like her father, Greg. Combined with her genetics, she loved to eat junk food, so she was on the heavy side. She was about five feet four and weighed 140 pounds. A feisty preteen, she talked back to our mother more than she should have even when our mother was obviously in mourning. I had to tell her more than once to stop being so disrespectful.

As I sat at my mother's kitchen table, I reflected on how my life had slowly transitioned from hungry nights and feelings of despair to finally having a car and money to buy groceries for me and my family. Growing up without things that I wanted and needed has taught me to be appreciative of what I have and to be humble and work hard. I also learned that many things can be difficult, especially when you are going through them, but the challenge will not last forever. Each difficult situation that my family and I went through prepared us for the next challenging situation by making us stronger as I reflected on how to handle similar situations in the future.

I recalled my now-deceased grandfather and the few times that my mother went to his apartment. She had been invited but at the same time was never really welcomed. My mother wanted to visit her father more often, but since she never felt comfortable around his wife, Little-Bit, her visits were limited mainly to those rare times when her stepmother was not home. James and I would go visit our grandfather not because we enjoyed seeing him but because our mother would send us there to ask for money for food. My mother used us as her messengers, but we didn't mind. She didn't want to go to Oscar's house and risk getting into a confrontation with Little-Bit, which would essentially guarantee that her request for money would be denied.

James and I got used to going to his apartment and didn't care if his wife was there or not. It may have bothered her that we were both taller than she was. She never said more than two or three words to us, mainly just, "Hello, boys," and when she said it, she seemed as if she was angry. I think that she was like an animal and could sense that we didn't like her. Shortly after we would arrive, she would go into the other room.

Each time I went to visit my grandfather, I can remember knocking on the door and being met by a cloud of cigarette smoke so thick that it looked like clouds in the sky. In the background was my grandfather with at least four of his friends sitting at the kitchen table gambling for money, playing a card game called Pitty Pat. There would be more money on that table than I was used to seeing. I wondered how my grandfather could have so much money and let his daughter struggle so much.

There wasn't a time that I went to his apartment when there wasn't music playing, and usually the song was "Green Onions" by Booker T & the MG's. That was, apparently, my grandfather's favorite song. Little-Bit would act cordially when they were playing cards. I guess that when he was winning money, she had nothing to complain about.

His funeral would be the second one of my lifetime. The first time, I watched as my grandmother was being put into the ground. I remembered the pain that I felt wondering how I would be able to get past losing her. It had been more than I thought I could handle at the age of ten. I hadn't known grief until her death introduced me to it. Now, at Oscar's funeral, the sadness I felt was mostly because I knew my mother was suffering.

My grandfather had life insurance, but Little-Bit kept all the money and gave my grandfather a bare-bones funeral that was one step up from a pauper's. I drove my mother, brother, and sister to a tiny church in Brooklyn for the funeral. By *tiny* I mean that if you had thirty people in this church, they would have been cited for overcrowding. There were three pews, a podium, and the casket. There was no piano—hell, there was no room for one.

Normally, funerals bring out family members that you don't often see, and this one was no different. There were a few cousins I hadn't seen in so long I didn't recognize who they were. Only two of my grandfather's five children were at the funeral—my mother and her brother Daniel. I surmised that my mother and uncle went to the funeral out of unconditional love and respect, not because they forgave him for how he was. My mother cried more than anyone else who was there. I sat there trying to comfort her. But the more I tried, the more she cried. I suspected she was crying because for so many years she wasn't a part of his life; and maybe if he was still alive, that could have changed. Now that he was dead, maybe my mother realized that the change that she had long hoped for would never happen.

I think that the emotional turmoil that she must have been feeling was intensified when she walked up to the casket and for the last time touched the man who had disappointed her. Seeing her crying over him angered me. Her tears brought up all the shit that my mother had gone through. When my mother was nineteen, she'd lost her older sister from kidney failure. Then, at twenty-nine, she'd lost her mother; and now her emotionally distant father, when she was only thirty-nine.

My anger then turned from my grandfather to my father and James's father, both of whom we'd never met and who hadn't been there for us just as my grandfather wasn't there for his children. As I sat there looking at my grandfather in the casket, I considered that I needed to stop blaming my father for not being in my life. My mother didn't tell him that she was leaving, and it wasn't fair to blame him for what she did. I would stop blaming him from now on. I had years of anger and loneliness inside, and something about the death of my grandfather caused me to open my eyes and heart and move on. My grandfather chose not to be a part of his children's life. I was determined that this cycle of abandonment, neglect, and emotional abuse had to stop. I promised myself that if I ever had children, I would forever be in their lives whether their mother and I stayed together or not.

On the outside, I appeared OK; but inside, I was angry throughout the rest of the funeral. I was bitter because I had to learn everything on my own. There were a lot of things that I got wrong before I got them right. And I had no one to lean on, not even my grandfather. I needed someone that I could learn from, but I didn't have that. Even though I didn't want to attend this funeral, it helped me make up my mind about finding my biological father. I was more determined than ever to find him. I needed to know why he didn't look for me. I wanted answers more than I wanted a relationship if that was even possible.

After the funeral, I took my family out to dinner at a local restaurant. We went to a well-known restaurant in Brooklyn called Junior's. Junior's Restaurant has been around since 1950, and they have some of the best cheesecakes in the world. With a full menu, you can order anything from burgers to chef's specialties. The restaurant is normally crowded, but lucky for us, the wait was only twenty-five minutes. The atmosphere was lively, and the staff was friendly. As we sat in the waiting area, we couldn't help but smell the wonderful aroma of the freshly baked cheesecakes. When they called us to be seated, my mother and James ordered their favorites: barbecue ribs, macaroni and cheese, and cabbage. I had salmon, broccoli, and rice; and Rhonda wanted a cheeseburger and fries, not surprisingly. Our dinner was topped off with some excellent strawberry cheesecake.

That was the first time we had dinner at a restaurant as a family; we had never been able to afford

Syrup Sandwiches

going out before now. I had my Navy pay, and James was working too, so we had a good dinner. We laughed and joked and talked about growing up in Brooklyn and how things had changed in our lives. The laughter and good food helped ease some of the hurt that my mother was feeling. That was certainly a day that none of us would forget.

Chapter 19
Husband Then Father

I was twenty years old, and in my mind, the hardest part of my life was behind me. Sure, the memories of all the pain stayed with me, but the days of sitting on the fire escape, running from a gang, or reliving the nightmares of Broadway Avenue were behind me. A new chapter in my life had begun, and I was growing into the man I wanted to become.

Going into the Navy turned out to be a great idea. It allowed me the opportunity to visit some of the most beautiful and remote places in the world. I could have never imagined that I would be walking down the streets of Palma, Spain, or visiting the Holy City of Jerusalem while in Israel. Barcelona was amazing. My ship was there for six days while we restocked supplies needed to distribute to the other ships in the battlegroup.

One of the benefits of being deployed on a supply ship meant that our port visits were usually longer than the other ships that deployed with us. A supply ship had to ensure that the logistics and coordination of all the supplies, including food and fuel for the other ships, were sufficient and readily available before we could leave a port. That meant that we would often be in port more than a week. Naples, Italy, was like our home port away from home. We spent a considerable amount of time there stocking the ship. Because we were in Italy for so long, I was able to tour Rome and the ruins of the

Colosseum, throw coins into the Trevi Fountain, and admire the architectural beauty of the Pantheon. Being able to travel the world was one of the perks of being in the Navy. The downside to being abroad meant that you were away from your family for extended periods.

Back then, our deployments were usually for six months. Today, they are longer, sometimes nine months. While being deployed, it wasn't uncommon for sailors to receive a *Dear John letter*. That was a letter you received from a significant other informing you that they were leaving you and the relationship was over. When you are in the middle of the ocean defending your country a thousand miles away, the last thing that you want is to be told that when you get back, the person you love will not be on the pier waiting for you. There have been sailors who couldn't take the pain of losing a loved one, especially when they couldn't see or speak to them to work out their situation. The sailor has no control of the situation and had to deal with the outcome of a one-sided decision. Sometimes sailors would commit suicide, usually by jumping overboard in the middle of the night. These situations are so common that ships have counselors on board to help sailors who receive Dear John letters. Still dating Wendy when I was deployed, I hoped that I would never receive a Dear John letter. Fortunately, I did not.

In May, when I was twenty-one years old, I asked Wendy to marry me. We had been dating for three years. We went to dinner; I gave her the engagement ring; I asked if she would marry me; and she said, "Yes." It was that simple. We didn't make a big deal out of the proposal.

Wendy had come from humble beginnings as I had. She'd also lived in Brooklyn but in a section called Williamsburg. Wendy had had the benefit of having both a mother and father who were married and lived together.

I was fascinated to find that out. Her father had passed away when she was fifteen. But until he died, he had been there for his three sons and five daughters.

That summer, Wendy and I, accompanied by one of Wendy's friends, went to the justice of the peace in New York City and got married. There was no expensive catering and no limos, no photographers, bridesmaids, or groomsmen. It was just the judge, Wendy's friend, who came as a witness, Wendy, and me. We wanted our families to attend the brief wedding, but city hall didn't allow more than four people in attendance.

Wendy wore a beautiful pink, draped-front dress that accentuated her shapely figure—she looked lovely. I wore a black double-breasted suit with a white shirt and black tie. Double-breasted suits were in style back then. I was nervous and sweating. It was also 92 degrees outside, which didn't help. Wendy was my first and only girlfriend. Now she was my wife.

What really attracted me to Wendy was her personality. She was kind, considerate, and thoughtful. She was quiet and soft spoken and had such a calming disposition, which is opposite from me. I loved Wendy. I decided to get married because I was committed to being there for Wendy. I also wanted the opportunity to have a family and to be a man who wouldn't ignore his responsibilities. I wanted to prove to myself and Wendy that I wasn't like all the men in my family. I would take all their mistakes and shortcomings and learn what not to do from them. I was determined to show love to Wendy and accept the love returned to me. I wanted to be the man of the house and have someone whom I could come home to, grow together with, and possibly have children with. I was determined that I would be the best husband that I could be.

We chose to not have a formal wedding because I was still living on a budget. My military salary was

$824 a month. I couldn't afford an expensive wedding. We did, however, have a large reception in the backyard of my mother's new apartment building. There were so many people there from my wife's side of the family. Her family was probably five times larger than mine. My favorite aunt, Lillie, and her children, Annette and Julie, were there along with my mother, brother, and sister. There were probably fifty people there, and there was enough food for people to take home.

My mother wore a yellow and white flowered sundress and was grinning from ear to ear when Wendy and I showed up. I had not seen her that happy in a long time. It was great just seeing her smile. She welcomed Wendy and her family with open arms. The reception was fantastic: We had a DJ who kept the music going and a bartender who worked for tips. The reception lasted until almost midnight. Wendy and I danced most of the night, and we enjoyed ourselves.

My mother no longer lived in the brownstone on Cornelia Street. She had moved into a building with twelve apartments. The owner of the brownstone was selling the building and my mother had to move out, so the city found her an apartment in the Bushwick section of Brooklyn. She would stay in this apartment building for twenty-six years before moving into a high-rise senior apartment.

Later that year, I found out that my high school, Alexander Hamilton Vocational and Technical High School, was considered the most troubled high school in New York City due to the combination of crime, poor student performance, and the dropout rates. It was closed by the Board of Education.

I had just graduated from there three years before. Sure, it was a terrible place, but I never thought that they would close it down. A member of the Board of Education was quoted as saying, "The dropout rate at

Alexander Hamilton is high. The school, in a building eighty years old, has an enrollment of 1,200; but only 135 students graduated in the previous academic year." The school was reopened under the name Paul Robeson High School for Business and Technology a year later. I am glad that I graduated when I did. I could only imagine how much of a nightmare it would have been to still be in school while they were trying to close it down and students were having to transfer to different schools.

I was on my first ship for almost four years. Now it was time for me to transfer to a shore command, which meant I wouldn't have to deploy out to sea and leave my family behind. I was still stationed in Virginia, so Wendy and I didn't have to move out of the apartment that we'd recently rented. At that time, the Navy was sending me back and forth to different training facilities that were in other states. Wendy was pregnant with our child, and as the due date got closer, we decided that it would be best that she go back to New York to stay with her mother.

In August, I received a call from Wendy's mother informing me that she had gone into labor. I was so excited. I told my mother-in-law that I was on my way to Brooklyn and that the drive shouldn't take me more than six hours since I was coming from Virginia. It was 9:30 in the morning. I figured I should be there no later than three-thirty or four that evening. I was driving a Gray 1980 Volkswagen Rabbit. I was driving slightly faster than the speed limit—OK, I was driving fast as hell. I made it to the New Jersey Turnpike and would be getting off on exit 13, the Verrazano-Narrows Bridge. When I got to exit 11 on the New Jersey Turnpike at Garden State Parkway, my car started slowing down and finally stopped. I thought I might have run out of gas, but then I remembered that I had filled the tank about an hour before. I was stuck on the damn New Jersey Turnpike.

Syrup Sandwiches

I was amazed at how many vehicles passed by me without even slowing down to ask if I needed any assistance. Finally, the state police showed up and called a tow truck to have me towed to the service area. My alternator had died and would cost $350 to replace. The broken alternator didn't concern me as much as the mechanic telling me that the part had to be ordered and would take about four hours to arrive. By the time that I got to Brooklyn Hospital, it was nine o'clock at night, and my son had already been born. I was disappointed that I didn't make it in time, but I was elated that he was a healthy boy and that my wife was doing well. My son, Tony, weighed seven pounds, eleven ounces; and he was twenty-one inches long, with brown eyes like his mother, and the longest hair I've ever seen on a boy. He had chubby cheeks like me. For the first time in my life, I could say that I was a father—now the hard part would begin.

I was only twenty-one when I got married and hadn't been with any other women. If my father or another responsible male was around, I would have asked for their advice. Was I too young? Should I have dated longer or even not have gotten married? As an adult, I can now look back and say that I did make the right decision to marry Wendy. If we hadn't married, there's no telling who I would be with now. I certainly wouldn't have my son, Tony, and Billie, my wonderful granddaughter.

When I held Tony for the first time, it was surreal. I couldn't believe that I was now a father. I had someone who would now look up to me, and I knew that I had to be the best father that I could be. I felt kind of lost because I allowed my thoughts to run away and started questioning myself. I wondered if I could be a good father. I didn't know anything about being a father, and I certainly didn't have any good examples in my life.

I was an immature twenty-one-year-old who was trying to learn how to grow up and at the same time trying to learn my role at parenting. Failure was not an option; I was all in, and I had to break the cycle of bad parenting that I was accustomed to.

As the reality of raising a child set in, I found myself often wanting to socialize with my friends, doing some of the things that young single adults often do. I hadn't been exposed to the party life as a teenager and was now captivated by the fun and excitement. So, I started hanging out with some of my Navy shipmates. We'd go to bars and clubs, sometimes drinking late into the night. I started to find myself wanting to be with my friends more than staying at home with Wendy and Tony.

I would sometimes get into arguments with Wendy about my hanging out. I remember one time a few shipmates and I went out drinking at a bar and stayed out until three in the morning. When I walked into the apartment, Wendy was still up.

"Why are you getting in so late?" I could tell that she was angry. "Where have you been?"

"I was hanging out with my friends at a few bars," I replied.

"You know you can't keep doing this. You need to grow up."

All I could say was, "OK."

But the time I most remember was when she said, "You can't keep going out so much. Tony needs you, and he didn't ask to come in this world."

When she said that, it was like a switch had been turned on. I immediately stopped getting ready to go out and turned around to face her. I slowly thought about how I was feeling at that exact moment. The emotions running through me were so powerful.

Finally, I said, "Wendy, you're right. Tony didn't ask to be in this world. That was our decision. I am sorry for not realizing what I've been doing to the both of you."

I felt bad that what I was doing had gotten to a point that I was, in a way, neglecting my only child and my wife. I thought about the feelings that I had had as a child without a father and how neglected I had felt. I realized that I had a lot of growing up to do and that I'd better get started. Providing for my family meant more than just paying bills and buying groceries, it also meant being emotionally supportive. I realized that neglect was a form of emotional abuse, and my son deserved better than that.

My biggest problem was that it was taking me too long to mature. I found it easier to want to stay out late at night partying than to stay home and be responsible for my family. I wasn't accustomed to the parenting or the party life. I realized that I couldn't effectively be a good parent if I chose to drink and socialize. I remember once when two of my Navy friends came to the apartment expecting me to go out with them drinking and partying, and as much as I wanted to go with them, I chose to stay home. I knew that my hanging out was becoming destructive, and the last thing that I wanted to do was cause problems for Wendy and Tony.

As I considered my situation, I knew I didn't regret having a child at a young age. I only regretted not knowing how to be a better parent. This was a turning point in my life. As I struggled to mature, I was taking a step in the right direction to become the father I was determined to be. I stayed home that night and thought about ways to be a more responsible father. I felt that this was another step toward becoming the husband and father I had determined to be all those years ago in Brooklyn.

Chapter 20
Searching for My Father

I decided that I would contact my Aunt Lillie and tell her that I was interested in finding my biological father. I wanted to know if she knew how I could find him. My aunt still had a lot of friends and some family members back in Georgia. One day, I mustered the courage to ask her.

"I will look into it for you," she said, "but I can't make you any promises. Don't get your hopes up too high."

By February of the following year, my aunt was able to locate some people who knew of my father and provided me with their contact numbers. I reached out to one of her contacts and they gave me my father's telephone number. Standing there, holding my father's phone number—a man whom I had never met, spoken to, or even known anything about—felt bizarre. The number was a Georgia number, and as I looked at it, I debated about whether I really wanted to dial it. *What if he doesn't want to talk to me?* I thought. I wondered if I was doing the right thing. I was now twenty-two, in the Navy, married, and a parent myself. I didn't need this man anymore. Still, I was determined that I had to reach out to him so that I could get some closure.

I dialed the number. Then I waited nervously as the phone rang.

After the fourth ring, a man answered, "Hello," in a raspy voice.

Syrup Sandwiches

Is this Walter?" I asked.

"This is Walter," he said.

"Walter, this is Anthony. I'm Rena's son."

After a long pause, he said, "Hello, son," like he'd been in my life since day one and was waiting to hear from me.

I didn't know whether to be upset or excited. We exchanged pleasantries, and then I got down to business. "Walter, it's good to finally talk to you. I didn't think that this day would ever come." Then I burst out, "It's been hard all these years, not knowing where you were, if you knew anything about me—why didn't you ever try to find me."

He said, "Son, when your mother left Georgia, she didn't tell me that she was leaving or where she was taking you. I didn't know where you were or how to contact you." His answer confirmed what my mother said. After talking to him, I was at peace with his answer and was willing to move on.

We spoke for about five minutes. I gave him my phone number, and we promised to stay in touch. I told him that I would be traveling to Alabama in June with one of my shipmates. I asked him if it would be OK if I came by to visit him on our way down South.

"That would be fine," he said and provided me with his address. Come to find out, shortly after my mother moved to New York, he had also moved from Dawson, Georgia. He told me he had moved to Hartford, Connecticut, which is not far from Brooklyn. But he stayed up North for only two years before moving to Atlanta, Georgia, where he lives to this day. We said our goodbyes, and all I could do was replay the entire conversation over and over in my head. This was so unreal, being able to finally speak with my father. But as I replayed the conversation with him, it hit me that my brother, James, still didn't know who *his* father was.

I picked up the phone and called my Aunt Lillie and thanked her for helping me locate my father. Then I asked her if she could reach out to her contacts in Georgia to see if they could locate James's father. I gave her all the information about James's father that my mother had given me, which was not much.

Once again, Aunt Lillie said, "I will look into it for you, but tell James I can't make him any promises and for him to not get his hopes up too high."

But I believed she'd do her utmost to find him. My Aunt Lillie loved me and would do anything for me. She had two daughters, and she would often tell me that I was the son that she never had. Every time she said that it melted my heart.

For the next few months, all I could do was think about the possibility of meeting my father. I was trying to figure out the real reason why I wanted to see him. I hated that he wasn't part of my mother's life and part of my life. Was I setting myself up for more heartache and disappointment? Was I looking for answers to questions that didn't have any answers? Would he lie to me or be honest about not being a part of my life for so long? I was working myself up and had to relax, or I was going to be a nervous wreck.

June had come and my shipmate Eugene Jackson and I were driving from Virginia to Alabama with a stop in Atlanta to visit my father. Eugene was a big country boy from Montgomery, Alabama. He had been in the Navy three years before me and had joined when he was twenty-one—unlike me, at seventeen. He said he had wanted to complete a few years of college before joining. He easily weighed 270 pounds. What made him look bigger was that he was five foot six. Eugene had light brown eyes that accentuated his short, jet-black afro. When he wore his Navy summer white uniform, he looked like a Sumo wrestler in a tight, white jumpsuit.

He knew that he was overweight by Navy standards, but no one would joke with him about his weight. They'd be afraid he would use his massive hands to pound them into the ground. People often moved out of his way when he approached, but they didn't realize that Eugene would go out of his way to help anyone.

There were times that I would feel bad for Eugene because other sailors would treat him differently because of his size. They would stare at him or secretly make jokes as he walked by.

I remember Eugene asked, "Hey, Skinny, do I look odd to you?"

"Dude, everybody looks odd to someone," I said. "Stop letting people get to you. Hell yeah, you look odd."

He slapped me on the back of my head and we both laughed.

I remember shortly after meeting Eugene; he introduced me to fishing. I had never fished before and instantly took a liking to it. There was something about fishing that relaxed me and allowed me time to think. I initially started freshwater fishing and then fell in love with saltwater fishing.

Eugene had an older brother named Peter, who also lived in Virginia. They sure didn't look alike. Peter was six feet and weighed about 180 pounds. And Peter acted nothing like Eugene. Peter seemed angry all the time. Eugene later confided in me that Peter was strung out on drugs and had left Alabama because his parents couldn't deal with his drug habit and kicked him out. Peter wouldn't go to rehabilitation or seek any other help for his addiction.

The ride to Georgia was long, and we took turns driving Eugene's car. Eugene drove a dark blue 1984 Pontiac Grand Prix with dark tinted windows. It was a beautiful car, but because I was so tall, the ride was uncomfortable. I had also gained a little weight. I was now 200 pounds. My broad shoulders and thin frame hid the weight, making me appear slimmer than I was, but during the long ride I regretted the extra bulk.

We finally arrived at the Atlanta, Georgia, address that my father had given me. As we approached the house that sat upon a slight hill, I could see seven adults and three children standing in the driveway waving us up.

As soon as we got out of the car, I met my father. We shook hands and hugged, then there was a moment of awkward silence. The silence was interrupted when one of the small children ran into me while playing in the yard.

I said, "Are you OK?"

"I'm OK, thanks," she replied.

She's so polite, I thought. Later, I would find out that the little girl was one of my cousins.

My father was tall but slightly shorter than me, probably six feet, two inches and about 220 pounds. He was dark chocolate and had a nicely trimmed beard and mustache. His eyes were dark brown like mine. He had a potbelly and wore a gray fedora. My first impression was that he seemed like a friendly guy. The strangest thing about seeing him was the stark resemblance that he and I shared. I really looked like him.

Both of my paternal grandparents were there to greet me. My grandfather was almost as tall as my father. He appeared to be in his early seventies, maybe younger, but it was hard to tell. It was obvious that he had aged well. He had sunken cheeks and a warm smile that made his smooth caramel complexion stand out with his thinly trimmed mustache. As the sun beamed brightly, his dark brown eyes and a healthy head of gray hair were exposed briefly under his tan-colored fedora.

He and my grandmother leaned up against a parked vehicle that was in their yard. My grandmother

Syrup Sandwiches

must have been in her late sixties. She was maybe five feet five. She was quiet and seemed as intrigued as I was. She had a short afro and a round face with fat cheeks like my father. She didn't smile much, at least initially. She gave me a long look. I think she wanted to make sure that I was really her son's offspring. Then she beamed and gave me a big hug. I bet she was convinced by seeing that her son and I looked so much alike.

She said, "Hello, son. Bend down." Then she kissed me on my right cheek. To say that I was surprised is an understatement. I didn't know what to say, so I muttered, "Thank you."

I met one of my brothers, Bob. Bob was handsome, about six foot one, slim, with a compelling smile. We shook hands and hugged. And immediately he started filling me in on our family history: "Including you, our father had a total of ten children from six different women," he said. "You're the oldest." I thought that ten children were a lot and that six different women was unimaginable but didn't say so. "You had four other brothers," he continued. "One of them, unfortunately, died some years ago. You have four sisters, and one of them is right over there." He pointed toward the house.

So, I met one of my sisters, Sylvia. She, too, was tall at five feet eleven. She was pretty with long beautiful hair and a very light complexion. She looked nothing like our father. We hugged, and she told me how exciting it was to finally meet me. I responded in kind.

I also met two uncles and three cousins. I spoke with all my family members and took pictures of each of them. I was pleased that I did have grandparents and looked forward to coming back to Georgia soon to get to know them better. My visit lasted about an hour. My father and I promised to remain in touch. I took a few more pictures of my new family and said my goodbyes. Then Eugene and I were on our way to Alabama.

This was an unbelievable experience: I finally met my father and his side of the family. I have grandparents and a bunch of brothers, sisters, uncles, aunts, and cousins. I looked forward to meeting all my family one day. I didn't get the opportunity to have the conversation that I needed to have with my father, as there were too many people around. It just wasn't an appropriate time. But I planned on having that one-on-one talk the next time we met. I started thinking that my father didn't try to find me because he was too distracted making babies by different women and wouldn't have had the time.

The two-hour ride to Alabama was short. I was trying to have a conversation with Eugene while trying to process what had just happened. It was overwhelming.

We arrived at Eugene's parents' house, and everything was completely different than what we'd just left in Atlanta. We were in the woods. There was no driveway, just a big yard full of pine trees that was littered with pine needles. I thought that I heard chickens. I turned around, and sure enough, chickens were running around like they owned the place. I had never seen a live chicken in my life. The house sat upon what looked like cinder blocks, and the chickens were running under the house and back toward us.

The entire house was made of wood, including the three steps leading up to the front door. There were a few holes in the front door, and you could look though the holes and see all the way through the entire house.

As Eugene started to walk his big ass up the steps, I could hear the wood creak, and my first thought was that he was going to break his parents' steps. I could only imagine that those steps weren't used to people like Eugene, but they held up, and he made it to the front

Syrup Sandwiches

door. I was afraid to go into the house because I feared the house would buckle under the extra weight.

But Eugene waved his hand at me and yelled, "Let's go!"

Hesitantly, I walked up the steps and into his parents' home. I could tell they were warm people and happy to see their son. They both gave him a big hug, and the father said, "Welcome home, son."

They looked at me, and before they could say anything, I said, "Hello, Mr. and Mrs. Jackson. It's a pleasure to meet both of you."

The father laughed at my formality. "Come over here, son, and give us a hug."

The house was clean and neat and had two small bedrooms. One was filled with boxes and furniture, and the other one must have been Eugene's room, as there were trophies and photos of him when he used to wrestle. There was one larger room for his parents, a kitchen, a family room, and a bathroom. I noticed one picture on the wall in the family room was of Eugene in his Navy uniform after graduation from boot camp. He had the biggest smile that I've ever seen from him. He looked so much younger and slightly thinner. There was another picture of Eugene, Peter, and their parents that sat in a curio cabinet. They all looked happy.

His mother prepared a fried chicken dinner with collard greens that were seasoned with ham hocks, some rolls made from scratch, potato salad, and some sweet tea—a traditional southern meal. I thought that I must have died and gone to heaven because the food was so delicious and divine. His mother prepared more than enough, which was amazing. Boy, Eugene sure can eat.

After dinner, Mr. Jackson gave me a serious look and said to me, "Son, I must apologize for not having enough room for you to have your own room tonight. We are using that room," as he pointed to a room full of the boxes, "for storage. You don't mind sleeping on the couch, do you?"

I smiled. "Mr. Jackson, I don't have a problem sleeping on a couch. Sleeping on a couch is a hundred percent better than sleeping on that thing they call a 'rack' in the Navy."

Eugene fell out laughing. Mr. Jackson looked relieved. What he didn't know was that I came from humble beginnings, and if I had to sleep on the floor, so be it. We stayed the night there. Eugene slept in his old room that he used to have when he was a child.

I don't think I slept at all that night. There were the animal sounds from outside and the house creaked which made me nervous. I kept thinking the whole place would collapse. On top of that, there was the excitement of having met some members of my long-lost family. Of course, I didn't sleep.

The next morning, we were on our way back to Virginia. Eugene mentioned his parents' house was known as a *shotgun house*. A shotgun house is one that is designed so that the rooms are laid out in a straight line and are connected without hallways. But at first, my stupid ass thought he meant the holes in the door were from a shotgun. Later I learned that my mother had also grown up in a shotgun house. Hell, I was born in one.

When I got back to Virginia, I called my mother and told her about my trip and about all the relatives that I had met and the many more that I would meet. For some reason, she didn't seem interested. I think that she might have been a little jealous. She might have thought I would now focus more attention on them and less on her and the family that I grew up with. I had no intentions of forgetting my immediate family in Brooklyn, and I had to make sure she knew that.

Syrup Sandwiches

I contacted my Aunt Lillie and told her about my trip to Atlanta and thanked her again for her help. She said that she couldn't find out anything about James' father and that she thought that it was likely that he'd died. I contacted James and told him the bad news about not being able to locate his father. Now he may never know if he has any family on his father's side. I felt bad for him, considering I had found my father and knowing that he, too, really wanted to find someone who was related to him.

When I told my mother about the news of James' father, she said, "I'm not sure if I had the right name of James' father. I think he may have given me a fake name when we met."

Are you kidding me? I thought. I'm sure the look on my face was priceless; it was a good thing that we were on the phone and my mother couldn't see my expression.

Less than a year after Eugene and I had returned from our trip to Georgia and Alabama, he was stabbed to death. Apparently, Eugene and his brother, Peter, were at the city park, and Peter wanted to borrow some money. Eugene told his brother that he didn't have any money, but his brother didn't believe him. They argued back and forth until Peter pulled out a knife and stabbed him to death. The news came as a shock to me and the other shipmates who were close to him. I was told that Eugene was stabbed twenty-nine times and didn't even make it to the hospital before he died. His brother was arrested.

Eugene's funeral was held in Alabama, and I couldn't bring myself to attend. I couldn't face Eugene's parents after he was killed. I felt a sense of responsibility for the safety of their son. Maybe I shouldn't have, especially since he was older. But I was so used to looking out for and caring for my brother and sister that

I had developed that same level of overprotectiveness for Eugene.

I couldn't believe that my friend was gone. He was my only friend at the time, and the pain of his death hit me hard. I became depressed. I had my wife and son to keep me company, but to lose a close friend was difficult. I wasn't prepared for his death. But who is ever prepared for death? I didn't know how to deal with my grief and found this extremely challenging. I tried to reach out to my father to talk to him and maybe clear some things up between us. I also wanted to possibly share my feelings about Eugene's death. He didn't answer when I called, so I left a message for him to contact me, but he never did. I would try a few more times before I gave up calling.

Two years later, my mother's youngest brother, Justin, died of AIDS. I was unable to attend the funeral, but my mother, brother, and sister attended. My Uncle Justin had lived in Queens, and we rarely saw him. He seldom came around to visit any of the family. It was almost as if he had forgotten that we existed. When he passed away, it didn't impact any of us too much, except maybe my mother, who was so sympathetic and forgiving. It bothered my mother that her baby brother didn't stay in touch. I remember one time after I joined the Navy asking her about him. "Rena, do you ever hear from Justin?" With sadness on her face, she replied, "Never."

Even though Justin was a half-brother to my mother, and they didn't share the same father, she loved him as she did her full siblings. That made me think about James and Rhonda, and that they, too, technically were my half-siblings. But that's not how I ever saw it. We had all grown up together, and they were all that I knew. We were blood. Now my family back in Georgia were also my half-brothers and sisters, but that felt distant. I knew hardly anything about them. We hadn't lived and grown up together. Nevertheless, I hoped that one day that I could feel much closer to them.

My sister Rhonda was giving my mother a difficult time. She was staying out late at night and coming home whenever she wanted. She was seventeen and living under my mother's roof. My mother told her to comply with her rules or move out. In November, Rhonda decided to move out. Rhonda was dating a guy who had no job, was living with his mother, and drank a lot. I don't know what she saw in him. I think that she was being spiteful toward my mother and didn't care whom she dated as long as she didn't have to conform to my mother's rules. Rhonda would come back to the apartment at random times of the day and night, and James would make sure that the door was locked. But my mother would then unlock the door so that Rhonda could get back in. James was frustrated with my mother for caving in and allowing Rhonda to do as she pleased even though she didn't live in the apartment anymore. While James and I didn't like the situation, there really wasn't much we could do about it. We just hoped that it wouldn't take too long before our mother insisted on the respect she deserved from Rhonda.

Chapter 21
Sunny Florida

It had been four years since I met my father's family. I had finished my first shore duty, and the Navy was stationing me and my family in Jacksonville, Florida. I welcomed the change of location. I was stationed on another ship—this time, an aircraft carrier. My wife and I found a gorgeous apartment that was only twenty-five minutes away from the base. I enjoyed having quick access to the base, but my wife had her eyes set on our buying a house. This was only our second apartment, but she wanted something that she could call her own.

"I am tired of living in apartments. I want my own house," Wendy told me.

I agreed, "It would be great to have a house. We can look for one when I return from my deployment." Wendy smiled and that made me feel good.

After arriving in Jacksonville, I was informed that my ship was already on deployment and that I would have to fly out to meet the ship. I left Jacksonville via military aircraft and eventually arrived on an isolated island called Diego Garcia, which is located seven degrees south latitude, off the tip of India. It is British Ocean Territory that the Navy uses as a launching point for operational forces deployed to the Indian Ocean and Persian Gulf.

Since my ship was in the Persian Gulf, I had to stay on the island for a few days until the ship could arrange to have me picked up. Diego Garcia was a small and beautiful island, and the view of the ocean was magnificent. The island was a prime location for fishing, and I loved to fish. I found myself fishing every chance I got. I caught grouper, snapper, and king mackerel. I even did some snorkeling while I was there.

One day while I was snorkeling, a few sailors came running toward me from the beach screaming, "Get out of the water!"

I asked what was wrong, and they told me that the waters were filled with barracudas. Needless to say, my days of snorkeling in Diego Garcia were over.

After three days of fishing and drinking, it was time to leave the island and head out to the ship. I sat in a minute airport waiting to fly out to the ship. Sitting next to me was this young sailor named Leon. I guess he didn't like the way that I looked at him because he looked back at me with a scowl on his face and said, "I will rip your head off and shit down your throat."

He extended his hand and introduced himself to me. I thought to myself, *this little guy must be crazy*. He was only about five eleven, maybe 160 pounds.

"I'm Anthony. Nice to meet you, I think," I replied, and we both smiled. I would later find out that Leon used to be in the Marines and was now in the Navy. I figured that ripping my head off shit must have been a Marine thing. He and I were both going to the same ship. Leon and I would wind up being the best of friends. Even to this day, I call him my brother. We flew out to the ship, and since it was an aircraft carrier, we landed on the flight deck.

Aircraft carriers are equipped with catapults which launch a plane at high speeds via cylinders filled with high pressure steam. Within a couple of seconds, the catapults can launch a plane up to 150 knots, the equivalent of 170 miles per hour, which delivered the speed and power needed for liftoff. When a plane returns to the aircraft carrier, it is caught by an arresting wire, which is a thick metal wire that the plane's tail hook catches to slow it for safe landing on the flight deck. Returning to the aircraft carrier in the middle of the open sea and trying to catch the arresting wire to land can be dangerous, especially if weather and ocean conditions are not optimal. If there is a storm or the water is rough and the pilot is not careful in landing, coming in too fast or landing too hard can be life threatening.

I was in complete awe at the size of the ship and the number of people and aircraft that were on it. When we landed, the crew had already been out to sea for 108 straight days without stopping for a port visit. They were angry and unfriendly. We walked to the berthing area, carrying our sea bags. We had a difficult time making our way through the crowded passageways, as the other sailors and marines were reluctant to give us enough room to walk by. They would push our sea bags as we walked past as if we were invading their personal space and looked at us as if they dared us to say anything. I understand now how they must have felt to be out to sea in the middle of the ocean for almost three and a half months without being able to walk on dry land.

We finally made it to the berthing area. The berthing area is the place where sailors sleep. The area is packed with racks that are normally stacked three high. Most of the racks open to provide storage for personal items and clothing. The berthing area is cramped, and privacy is just a wish. I worked in the Communications Department. Leon worked in the Aviation Department, and we would see each other when we could. We would talk about life onboard the ship and how we couldn't wait to get back into port.

"I don't think I like this shipboard life," he said.

I was used to living on a ship, so it didn't bother me too much. "It'll get better, you'll see," I replied.

Syrup Sandwiches

Living on an aircraft carrier while deployed out to sea is like living on a floating city. There were people from all walks of life and from all over the world. I really loved the diversity and being able to interact with people who had different backgrounds, cultures, and beliefs. I learned so much from people who were not from Brooklyn or even the United States for that matter. The more I spoke and interacted with people from all over the world, the more I realized that I had a lot to learn. I started to think that the Navy had become a blessing for me. I was now being exposed to so much more than I could have possibly imagined.

The cruise was six months long, and we were in port for fifteen days during the entire deployment. Being on deployment was now more difficult for me because I was leaving behind my wife and son and felt as if I was, in some ways, abandoning them. I knew that I was away defending the country and providing for my family, but I could not escape feeling that I was somehow neglecting them. Wendy would write a letter almost daily and would send pictures of Tony as he was growing up. I wasn't home when Tony took his first steps or when he spoke his first words. It was moments like those that made me feel confused. I was happy that my son was growing up, but then I was sad that I couldn't be there to see it.

I sometimes got the opportunity to call home from the ship's amateur radio, also referred to as a *ham radio*. The amateur radio operated over the amplitude modulated (AM) frequency, and reception was often sporadic at best. When I spoke to Wendy, we would have to say "over" after each sentence. That was the best form of communications that we had back then on the ship.

I remember so many times during my calls, I would say, "Hello, Wendy, how are you and Tony doing? Over."

She'd reply, "We're doing fine, just missing you. Over."

This would go on the entire time of the conversation, normally lasting only a minute or two.

Deployments had been less stressful for me when I wasn't leaving behind Wendy and Tony. To this day, it amazes me when someone can't accept their spouse leaving for a week or two at a time for work, so they decide they want to get divorced. Being separated for extended periods of time is one of the primary reasons some people decide to end their relationship. It is unfortunate that the relationship often ends while the service member is away from home and is unable to do anything to prevent the breakup. Knowing that you are out to sea and are unable to sit down and have a face-to-face conversation with your family makes deployment even more depressing.

Coming to the realization that the person with whom you once shared your heart, time, love, and money is no longer there for you can be emotionally traumatic. Lying in your rack at night in the middle of the ocean and thinking that you will no longer receive letters, care packages, or occasional phone calls can sometimes be too much for a sailor to deal with. I've seen shipmates who received Dear John letters telling them that their spouse left with the children and took everything. This happened to my friend, Charles Watson. He received a letter while we were deployed, and his wife told him that she could no longer deal with him going out to sea and being away from home so much. I remember Charles crying like a baby, and there was nothing that I could do or say to make him feel better. I gave him a brotherly hug and just let him cry until he stopped. I felt terrible and prayed that his wife would change her mind.

There were many other married shipmates who would be returning home to face an empty apartment or house. It was hard not to feel sorry for the ones who had their lives turned upside down while on deployment. After receiving news that your wife is leaving you and taking the kids, it's almost impossible to perform your daily shipboard tasks, interact with people, and stay motivated or have any enthusiasm or desire. Charles's wife didn't change her mind; and when he returned to the house that they had shared, she, his child, and all their belongings were gone.

I can understand how difficult it must be for the spouse of a sailor to have their mate gone for so long, but it would probably not be as traumatic if the couple could at least talk about it before or after the deployment, not while the sailor is away.

When I returned from deployment, Wendy and I immediately began looking for a house. We found an area on the south side of Jacksonville where developers were building new homes. We were able to find a home that would be built for $89,000. After applying for my Veterans Administration (VA) loan and going through all the paperwork, we were approved to purchase a home. We were elated and amazed to be able to purchase a home, considering that up until then we both had always lived in apartments. The construction would only take four months. Wendy and I would go over to the house while it was being built and take photos. It was amazing to see all the work that goes into building a house. When our ranch house was completed, it had a two-car garage, a large backyard, three bedrooms, and two and a half baths. This was a significant achievement for us, and I was in a happy place in my life now especially since I only had one more deployment to complete in the Mediterranean Sea before it was time to go on shore duty.

I had completed all the classes for my associate degree. Shipboard life can be challenging, rewarding, and depressing. One of the benefits of being stationed on a large ship like an aircraft carrier was the ability to take college classes while deployed. I took full advantage of the opportunity, taking as many classes as I could. Most of my classes were from the basic disciplines: science, social studies, arts and humanities, and mathematics.

I remember when I told my mother that I had earned my degree, she started crying. I didn't like it when my mother cried even if it was for something good. Her crying takes me back to the times when she had no other option than to cry, hoping that things would somehow get better. And I wasn't used to her crying tears of happiness.

I said, "Rena, please don't cry."

Then she had the gall to say, "Boy, I'm not crying."

We both laughed, and she told me how happy and proud she was of me and that I was the only one in the family that she knew of to have a degree. Myself, I didn't think much of it. It was only an associate degree. Little did she know, I had plans to go much further. I had gotten a taste of higher education and now I was hooked. I called James to tell him the news about my degree, and he, too, was happy and proud of me. After that, James told me he had proposed to his girlfriend. I asked, "Are you marrying Mary?" I was already guessing the answer but having been deployed, I was wanted to make sure nothing had changed.

While I was deployed, I didn't have any contact with anyone other than Wendy, so I couldn't keep up with all the family news. But it was delightful to know that my brother was about to tie the knot. I knew little about his girlfriend and looked forward to getting to know her better. I had noticed the few times that I saw

Syrup Sandwiches

her, she would want to be the one in control and would give James a certain look that would stop him in his tracks. He would look at her as if asking for her approval to continue.

I gave James my blessing and told him that my family and I would be at his wedding. James was twenty-three then and still living at home with our mother. It was a good thing that he was gainfully employed as a manager at a department store and was helping her with the bills. Now that he was about to get married and would be moving out, my mother would be living by herself. Well, mostly, Rhonda was still coming and going at will anytime she wanted.

James and Mary had a large and beautiful wedding with bridesmaids, groomsmen, a photographer, and great food—all the things that Wendy and I didn't have when I got married. Mary was going to have a big wedding, no matter how much debt James would amass. The reception was enjoyable, and James seemed happy, so that was good enough for me. I just hoped it would last.

A week after James's wedding, while he and his wife were away in Jamaica, my mother called me to tell me that her sister Denise had died. Denise had been helpful to my mother, especially during the blackout. She'd welcomed us when our apartment building was being vandalized and burned and let us stay with her. Over the years, she had invited us over to dinner and was kind to my mother and us. She was there for us when we really needed her. I knew that my mother was having a difficult time dealing with her death. Hell, Denise had been her oldest living sister. We knew that my aunt was dealing with some health issues but hadn't realized how severe they were. She died of a massive heart attack.

I couldn't believe I was twenty-eight and on my way to another funeral. My aunt's funeral was at the same tiny church where my grandfather's funeral had been held. The church was the same as it was seven years ago; nothing had been done to improve or expand it. There were more people at this funeral than at my grandfather's. Denise's son, Kem, was there. I hadn't seen him more than twice in the past ten years since he was in the Army and stationed in Germany. The service was quick, and my aunt was buried in the same cemetery in New Jersey where her sister, mother, and father had been buried.

    James moved out of my mother's apartment shortly after getting married. He and his wife found a two-bedroom apartment in another section of Bushwick. They lived there for two years before they welcomed their first child. My brother was thrilled to have a daughter.

    Rhonda was still coming and going in and out of my mother's apartment as she'd been doing for the last four years. She was now pregnant by her loser boyfriend. She was still working as a security guard, for very little pay. Now she had a child to feed and a boyfriend who couldn't hold down a job. She relied on my mother to help provide for her and the child. James and I weren't happy about Rhonda using our mother like that, but there was nothing that we could do. I really believed that my mother enjoyed her daughter and the baby needing her. I guess that since she had an empty nest, she welcomed the company. Almost three years later, Rhonda would have her second child, a son, by the same guy.

    Once she had two children, her boyfriend decided that he no longer wanted to be in a relationship with her. He kicked her out of his mother's apartment, where she had stayed off and on. So, she moved back in with our mother for the long haul.

Chapter 22
Back to Virginia

My last three years in Jacksonville on shore duty went better than I could have imagined. I was looking forward to staying in Jacksonville and possibly finishing my career there. I was advancing in my naval career, and Wendy was happily working at a bank as an auditor. Tony was eight years old and doing well in school. He loved playing baseball and skateboarding. I was also working part-time jobs, such as selling beepers and pagers and doing door-to-door sales giving in-home vacuum cleaner presentation for additional income, in between taking classes at a local college. Even though things were looking good, I was having a problem managing my Navy life, second job, studying, parenting, and being a husband. I had allowed myself to become overwhelmed. I was trying to do too much.

There would be times when I would come home in a bad mood and wouldn't want to talk to my wife or son. Strong and understanding, Wendy allowed me some space. But my son needed more from me. I was so wrapped up in trying to provide financially for my family that in some ways I wasn't there for Tony. The Navy was stressful and demanding, even on shore duty. I had to figure out how to balance my work life and my home life. Even at thirty years of age, I was still learning and trying to mature. Wendy and Tony didn't like fishing, so sometimes I would go fishing by myself. Fishing gave me the time to relax and reflect on my life. I would fish and think.

Time was going by fast, yet I could remember what it was like when I was just a teenager growing up in Brooklyn. Who would believe I'd be sitting here in the backyard of my own home, drinking a glass of Crown Royal on the rocks, staring into the sky, thinking how blessed I was? But it was time to change duty stations again. My three-year tour of duty at the Jacksonville, Florida, naval base was about to end, and it was time to contact the Navy detailer to see if they could find a duty station here for me in Florida. The Navy detailer is an advocate for the sailor. They try to match the available billets with the personnel who have the required skill sets.

I just knew with all the ships in the area that my detailer would be able to find something for me. But he couldn't. I was informed that he was unable to find any duty stations that would keep me in Florida and that I would be stationed back in Norfolk, Virginia, even though I practically pleaded with the detailer to let me stay in Florida. I had so much going on. My family and I were doing well, at least outwardly, and I didn't want to upend our lives.

The detailer didn't seem impressed with, or concerned about, what was going on in my personal life. He said again, "You're going back to Norfolk, Virginia, on a ship."

The decision had been made. I had no other choice than to move back to Norfolk, Virginia. I had to break the news to my wife and son that we would be moving. They were both heartbroken. My son started to cry because he would be leaving all his friends and classmates. I felt bad for my family, but what were my choices? Get out of the Navy and end my career of thirteen years or move to Norfolk? There was no way that I would throw away that many years in the Navy just

Syrup Sandwiches

to stay in Florida. We would just have to move back to Virginia and start all over. My wife would be able to find work; and my son was smart—he'd do well in his new school and meet new friends.

Sadly, we were unable to sell our home before it was time to move. My realtor suggested that I let someone assume my Veterans Administration (VA) loan, and that's what I did. Shortly after that, Wendy and I were no longer homeowners.

Back in Virginia, I was stationed on another aircraft carrier. Because of my height, aircraft carriers better suited me; I didn't have to duck down as much as I walked throughout the ship. There was a time when the detailer stationed me on a small ship, a minesweeper. The ship was so small, I was unable to walk anywhere on it without ducking. The sailors onboard would stare at me as I was almost bent in half trying to make my way throughout the ship. Once the commanding officer of the ship saw that I was too tall for the ship, he immediately contacted the Navy detailer, and I was removed from the ship within three weeks.

Things in Norfolk, Virginia, had changed a lot since 1988. There were stores that were open on Sundays, the highways were repaired, and the area was starting to look like a city that had potential. We were able to rent a lovely townhome in the Virginia Beach area in a good school district.

Tony, now ten and in the fifth grade, quickly adjusted to his new school and made some new friends. His grades were great, and he was excelling in all his classes. Wendy was able to find a job at a local cable company as a fraud analyst. All was well. My ship wouldn't be deploying for another year, so that gave me time to enroll in the local college to continue working toward my bachelor's degree.

My ship's deployment date to the Mediterranean Sea came sooner than I wanted, and once again, it was time to leave my family behind while I defended my country. Saying that I defended my country made me feel better about leaving.

Wendy and Tony were on the pier to see me leave. I gave my son a big hug and kissed him on his head and then hugged and kissed my wife goodbye. It was hard to leave them as I headed toward the ship to board and depart, already feeling lonely and missing my family. I wasn't the father and husband that I wanted to be. I was a work in progress, and I was determined to get better. The biggest problem that Wendy and I had was my inability to mature fast enough. I didn't know how to be a good husband and didn't have any examples in my family. I was learning and making mistakes as I grew. I also had difficulty expressing my feelings. It was challenging for me to say how much I loved someone even if I showed them. My mother was like that too. She always showed us love, but we rarely heard her say it.

The pier was filled with families saying their last goodbyes, hugging, and kissing before watching their loved ones disappear into the gray metal floating city. Children ran after their parents with tears in their eyes, yelling, "Daddy!" or "Mama, don't leave!"

We stood on the flight deck in our dress uniforms, waving to the crowd as the ship was towed out into the open waters, not to be seen again until six months later. To feel better, I started to think that my leaving might be a good thing for Wendy and Tony. After all, I was still struggling with learning how to be a better husband and father. I'd noticed that my son was hanging out more with his friends. Was he avoiding me and my sometimes-bad mood? The Navy had taught me discipline, structure, rigidness, how to conform, and how

Syrup Sandwiches

to follow orders. Now, as Tony was growing older, I was bringing more of that home with me. I had become stricter with my son and found it difficult to find the balance between the level of strictness required with my shipmates and the lesser level my son needed. The line between the Navy and my family had become blurred.

Fortunately, this would be the last ship that I would have to be on before retiring after twenty years of service to my country. Some people chose to stay in the Navy longer than twenty years. I was determined to do my twenty years and not a day more. I had become tired of leaving my family and wanted to have a stable life, not wave goodbye from the flight deck of a ship that would be gone for months.

Ships that are on the East Coast normally deploy to the Mediterranean Sea, and West Coast ships normally deploy to the Pacific Ocean. During the cruise we had port calls in Spain, Greece, Italy, France, and Turkey. Six-month deployments can go by fast, depending on the number of port visits that you have and the length of time at each port. Good thing for me, we had enough port visits to help ease the loneliness of missing my family.

However, my son was growing up fast without me. In some ways, I felt that I was doing what I had to do to provide for him so that he could have all the things that I never had and even one day be a better man than I was. Then there were times that I wondered if I was causing more harm by being away from him so much even though being away was due to my job. I had to reason with myself. My father hadn't been there for me, and I'd survived. I was trying to make something out of myself. I was active in my son's life. But there were times when I was home with my son and still felt as if I was away.

As the deployment neared its end, the excitement on the ship was electrifying. Everyone on board was jubilant, talking about all the things that they had planned for their return.

Before we made it back to Norfolk, I was in the galley having lunch, *chow*, as we call it in the Navy and my supervisor came to my table and said, "Stop eating now and come to the office," and walked off.

His request seemed odd. I knew that I hadn't done anything wrong. The way that he said it in front of the other shipmates appeared rude and disrespectful, so I didn't immediately leave the table. I finished my meal first.

On my way to the office, the supervisor met me in the passageway and stood directly in front of me. I moved to the side of him to pass him, and he immediately said that I had pushed him. He put me on report and tried to get me into trouble. Fortunately, he didn't have any proof or witnesses supporting his claim, and I was given a warning.

That was the second and last time that I had any disciplinary problems while in the Navy. Maybe the supervisor didn't like me because he and I would often disagree, but I never thought that he would take it to a level that it might affect my career.

We had *four days and a wake-up*—that's a military expression which means we had four days, plus the last day when we would leave or "wake up" on high alert, before arriving back to our home port of Norfolk. Sleeping was out of the question. We were too anxious and wired to sleep, so some of the sailors and I would stay up late into the night playing cards and talking shit.

On homecoming day, the tugboats slowly guided us through the channel and into port. We were standing on the flight deck in our dress whites. We could see the crowds on the pier. They looked like a bunch of ants. As the tugboats pulled us closer, faces became clearer. It looked like hundreds if not thousands of people screaming and yelling, "Welcome home!"

We were all excited onboard the ship and would stay on the flight deck until the ship was completely tied to the pier and we'd hear over the loudspeaker, "Secure from manning the rails." At that point, everyone would scurry throughout the ship, waiting for their turn to leave and be reunited with their loved ones.

When it was my turn to go ashore, I was happy to see my wife and son on the pier as soon as I departed the ship. They both greeted me with big hugs. As we embraced, time stood still.

"Welcome back, Dad," Tony said.

Hearing those words, I couldn't contain my excitement. I was elated to be back home. It was great to be back and to be able to spend some real time with the family. Now that I was back, I had to focus on my relationship with my son. Tony was eleven and growing fast. I couldn't believe how much my son had grown in only six months. He was three inches taller, and his voice was a little deeper.

Three weeks later, I took a trip to Brooklyn to visit my mother and sister and to enjoy some of that great Brooklyn food that I loved so much. I had been to many places abroad and in the United States, but there was no place like Brooklyn. We still had the best pizzas, subs, and franks. The dance clubs were electrifying, and we had every kind of sports team imaginable. We also had Manhattan and the nonstop city life.

Brooklyn was different for me now because I wasn't poor. When you have enough money to buy fun, life changes. I was no longer confined to taking trains and buses for transportation or making sandwiches out of condiments. I wasn't financially strapped; however, I was still a long way from being wealthy.

My sister was twenty-three, working as a security guard, and still living with my mother. Hadn't my mother spoiled Rhonda since she was born? But I could see that my mother enjoyed having someone in the apartment with her. My mother was now fifty-one years old, single, and not dating.

Chapter 23
Get Out

It had been four months since I had returned from deployment. One day after leaving work, when I got to the front door of our townhouse, there was an eviction notice on the door. My first thought was that there was no way we could be getting evicted. We always paid the rent, and it was never late. After the shock of seeing an eviction notice on my door wore off, I contacted the property management company that we were paying our rent to so that I could find out what was going on. I was told that the owner of the townhouse had not been paying the mortgage company and that the house was in foreclosure. The management company said that they were sending my payments to the owner, but the owner wasn't paying the bank. They were giving us a month to move out.

Remembering the poverty of my childhood, I just shook my head at the irony of being evicted now when I was financially stable and had no problem paying my rent. I wanted to scream and then choke the hell out of the owners, not necessarily in that order. Wendy and I had to scramble to find an apartment in a month. Wendy was a lot calmer about the situation than I was, and she would tell me, "Don't stress out. We'll find something."

It was her calmness that helped me stay focused. It was a terrible situation because we would have to find a place, come up with the first month's rent and a deposit, and then get a moving truck and somehow move an entire townhouse full of furniture. It took almost three weeks to find an available apartment that was affordable and in an attractive neighborhood.

Fortunately, we found a lovely townhome in another part of Virginia Beach. A few of my shipmates helped me move into the townhome, which was actually bigger and better than the previous one. The rent was higher, but this townhouse was more attractive and in a better location.

By the time I left my last ship, I had racked up a eleven years and ten months of total sea time, which meant that out of the seventeen years that I had been in the Navy, more than eleven of those years had been spent out to sea away from my family. I couldn't wait to be done with the shipboard life and the Navy for that matter. I only had three more years.

It was 1998. I would remain in Norfolk, Virginia, my last shore duty assignment for the next three years. I would be doing anything and everything to prepare myself for civilian life. I was almost done with my bachelor's degree. My focus was on preparing for what life would look like once I was no longer in the service.

Just before I was ready to retire from the Navy, we decided it was time to buy a home. Wendy and I had been in our townhouse for almost five years and we were looking forward to purchasing a home. We found some new homes that were being built in Virginia Beach and decided to purchase a new home there. It took five months to build the house. This house was bigger than the one that we had built in Jacksonville. It was a two-story home, not a ranch-style home. Like the home in Jacksonville, it had a two-car garage, but it had four bedrooms, two and a half baths, and a decent-sized backyard. Once we had moved and settled in, I could focus my attention on retirement.

The Navy provided a class called The Transition Assistance Program (TAP), which provided information, tools, and training to help service members and their spouses get ready to successfully transition from the military life to civilian life. It was a weeklong class that provided insight on how to prepare your resume and offered helpful tips on the hiring and interview process in the civilian community. They also provided helpful information on how to dress for success and to be ready to not only look your best but how to represent yourself professionally. This class was an invaluable opportunity to make sure that you were ready for civilian life as it provided the necessary tools to help make the transition as seamless as possible.

Planning for my retirement ceremony was also an enormous undertaking. There were a ton of things that had to be taken care of beforehand such as arranging guest speakers, picking out the eight sideboys, rehearsals for everyone involved in the ceremony, and several other things. *Sideboys* were members of an even-numbered group of military personnel posted in two rows at the quarterdeck or gathering place for a formal ceremony, such as a retirement ceremony or change of command ceremony.

The number of details involved in planning a retirement can be stressful, requiring a great deal of preparation and coordination similar to planning for a formal wedding, I imagined. I wanted the ceremony to be quick, and I wanted to make sure that I did everything I could to ensure that my guests would enjoy themselves. I was thinking that I only had one more year before my retirement and how different it would be to not be in the military after twenty years.

My thoughts were interrupted by a phone call from my mother. Her brother, my uncle Daniel, had died.

Uncle Daniel was physically abusive, beating every woman he ever dated. I remember Uncle Daniel as an enraged man clutching a Bible. I knew he was battling something internally in his mind. At his funeral he lay in the same small church where his other relatives had been laid to rest. As I looked down at my uncle in the casket, my first thought was to be angry at him for being abusive and a terrible father. Then I realized that he had deep-seated emotional issues and never did anything to address them. I would not allow his mental issues to incense me. I asked myself, *will he, too, be in a better place?*

When I returned home from the funeral, I resumed thinking about my retirement plans. I had to determine the location and time of the retirement ceremony. I chose a chapel that was located on the naval base. It was an average-sized chapel, which was large enough to accommodate up to 150 people. That would be more than enough space for the ceremony that I had planned. I wasn't expecting more than fifty people.

I wanted my mother to come to the retirement, but her health wasn't getting any better with her asthma and her high blood pressure not under control. She didn't want to travel, and I did not expect my sister to attend. However, James said that he would drive down from Brooklyn. The more that I thought about the ceremony, the more nervous I became. The closer that my retirement got, the more my anxiety increased. James arrived three days before my ceremony and was as excited as I was. My wife and son were looking forward to my leaving the military and being home more often— I was too! My time of serving my country was almost over, and now it was time to start a new life. I had given all that I could to the Navy, and I was ready for this change, even if I didn't have a clear direction of where I was headed. I was emotionally ready and would make sure that I worked on my second career as thoroughly and diligently as I did my first one.

Chapter 24
Bye-bye, Navy

It was Friday and Retirement Day was finally here. I was beaming from ear to ear but nervous. I would be standing in front of forty-six people who were anxiously waiting to see me. All eyes were on me, and I had to be perfect. I had rehearsed my speech at least a hundred times and still wasn't sure if I could deliver the speech that I had planned. As with most retirements, mine started with the National Anthem. My singer was extraordinary; my guests swayed and smiled as she sang her heart out.

The invocation was longer than I wanted or expected. I guess the preacher forgot that I had only rented the chapel for two hours. The presiding officer made up for it because he spoke as if he was double-parked and had to go move his vehicle before he got a ticket. He spoke very fast, and I think English was his third language because I sure as hell didn't hear much English.

The guest speaker was a good friend of mine and he spoke from the heart, revealing all my character flaws like the fact that I was impatient, bullheaded, and a pain in the ass sometimes. He also said that I was the only person that he had ever met who had consistently treated all people with respect and kindness and that I would give them the shirt off my back if they needed it. I almost cried when he said that because I have lived by the mantra that I would always do unto people as I would have them do unto me. I believed that if I was thoughtful and kind to everyone, people would reciprocate. It didn't always work out that way, but I continued to believe and practice that belief no matter what and I still do so today.

During the ceremony, my wife and son were both given a Certificate of Appreciation from the United States Navy for their unselfish, faithful, and devoted service during my military service. They were both proud of me and accepted their awards with honor. They had endured a great deal of heartache and loneliness during my deployments. It wasn't easy for my wife to raise our son alone and do a wonderful job, especially the difficult, unpredictable, and challenging times. I loved her for that. I also loved her for not sending me a Dear John letter when so much time alone felt unbearable. I was given a Certificate of Appreciation from the state of New York by Governor George Pataki, a congratulations letter from the President of the Borough of Brooklyn, Howard Golden, and a Joint Service Commendation Medal from the Navy.

Now it came to a point in the ceremony when it was my time to speak. I had rehearsed my speech to exhaustion, and I was ready. I spoke about who I was and where I grew up, the duty locations where I served, my family life, and my accomplishments. And finally, I was about to thank everyone for their support and attendance. I was determined not to cry. I had seen some of the most durable and rigid people retire, and at the end of their touching and emotional speech, they would often break down and cry. Some cried like a baby and had to be assisted from the podium. I was determined not to be a part of the "always-strong-but-weak-at-the-end" crew. But suddenly, tears started falling from my eyes. I tried hard to be tough, but there was something about leaving a group of people that had been there for you for so many years and now you have to say goodbye to them and the organization. I'd never been a part of anything for that long in my life. When you've served twenty or more years with a group of people that you call family and that you've gone to battle with and would die for, it isn't easy saying goodbye to them. The Navy had been a major part of my life and had provided a career that had helped sustain and provide for me and my family and had opened doors for greater endeavors.

I was thirty-seven and now retired. I was still young and had my whole life in front of me. For the last twenty years, I had worked nonstop and had a few part-time jobs in between. Now, I was unemployed, and my Navy retirement wasn't enough to live off. I needed to find another job. I thought I would take about three weeks off, relax, and enjoy my free time—but I was wrong.

After one week of not working, I couldn't take it anymore. I was so used to working since I was a child, and to suddenly not work seemed strange. Sure, it would have been great to take some much-needed time off, but my mind wouldn't let me take a break. I had to work. I applied for work at a local Lowe's Home Improvement Store. Fortunately, I was hired immediately for the Electrical Department since I had an electrical background, having completed an electrical program at an online technical college earlier in my Naval career. I wasn't working there longer than two weeks before I was called to work for a government contractor. I would be hired as a lead technical engineer for a major defense contractor. I was stoked.

Shortly after my retirement, I sat Tony down and had a conversation with him. I wanted to know what his plans were when he finished high school. He only had one year left in school, and I wanted to make sure that he was preparing for his future. Until this point, whenever I asked about what he wanted to do after school, he'd say, "Dad, I have time," and suggested that he would probably go to college. He told me that joining the military was out of the question.

I then asked, "What's wrong with the military?"

He said with conviction and a scowl, "Dad, I could never leave my family like you did." Then he gave me a hug to lighten up the mood, I guess.

I don't think that Tony was trying to be mean about what he said, but at that moment I felt bad—not for what he said or how he said it—because I understood how he felt and what he meant. My being away from him while he was growing up, especially during his early years, was tough for him, and he'd felt neglected. I felt the same neglect when *my* father wasn't around. His situation and my situation were different, though. I didn't know my father or his whereabouts. But the effects were similar. I wasn't there for Tony many times when he needed me just as my father hadn't been there when I needed him.

My son then said, "Dad, I used to stay away from home a lot because I knew that you were dealing with something in the military. Even though you were mean and overly strict, I gave you a pass because I knew that you were under a lot of pressure when you were going in and out to sea."

I was flabbergasted. I didn't know if I was more upset with myself for treating my son like that or relieved that he found a way to cope with all my shortcomings. I think it was a little of both.

"Tony, I am really sorry for all of the pain that I have caused you and your mother while I was in the Navy," I told him. "I love you, and I meant to be there for you when you needed me. I apologize. And now that I am out, I promise to be the best father ever. I'm here for you."

I could understand my son's resentment toward the military. But, in many ways, the Navy was my father. It had given me direction, guidance, discipline, and support. Later that night as I lay in bed, I couldn't help but ponder the conversation Tony and I had had. I knew that I wasn't there for him for a significant portion of his childhood, and that conversation showed me that my being away from my son had had a negative impact on him. There was nothing that I could do to get back the time that was spent away from him, but I knew that I would do everything that I could to ensure that I was there for him now. I couldn't continue to fail my only child.

Tony graduated from high school and enrolled in a community college. He had planned out his higher education, and he wanted to go to a community college before going to a four-year university.

That same year, my brother James decided to move his family out of Brooklyn to a place that was safer for his four girls. He wanted a place that might have better schools and a slightly lower cost of living, so he and his wife moved to a home in New Jersey. It was a newly renovated, three-story house with three bedrooms and two and a half baths, a beautiful backyard, and plenty of needed space for his children to play.

One time I remember calling James on the phone while I was in Virginia and told him that I wanted to come to New Jersey so that he and I could hang out together for our joint birthday. He agreed, and I told him I'd be there in two days. It would be fun to hang out with my brother. We hadn't done that in a long time, and I was looking forward to conversation with him about a lot of things. Two days later, on Saturday morning, I drove the five and a half hours to New Jersey. I arrived at James's house at eleven in the morning. When I got to his house, James and his wife had already been arguing. James had a look on his face as if he was saying, "Man, I'm sorry." I didn't know what the look was about, so I sat there and tried to act as if I wasn't listening to him, and his wife go back and forth about today being his birthday and how he was going to hang out with me.

Next thing I know, James tells me that his wife wanted to take him out for his birthday and that they'd be back soon. I assumed that she wanted to take him somewhere to get something to eat and they'd be back after that. They didn't come back until seven hours later. When they returned, they were still arguing. At this point, I knew that James wouldn't be able to go anywhere with me. I was so hurt that all I could do was get back in my car and drive back to Virginia. The drive back home to Virginia was a long one. It was my birthday, and I'd spent most of my time on the road—to say I was angry was an understatement.

Wendy and I became empty nesters when Tony moved out of our house and into a home that he and some of his friends rented together in Virginia Beach. Tony is an avid skateboarder with some big-name sponsors. He is well known in the skateboard community. When Tony turned twenty-three, he decided to move to California to pursue his passion for skateboarding. Tony returned two years later and enrolled in Old Dominion University to major in business marketing. After receiving his bachelor's, he went on to William and Mary and completed his master's in business. I'm proud of my son, and I made sure that I told him that. I would say jokingly, "Son, look at you trying to be like your father," and we would both laugh; Then I'd say, "I'm very proud of you. Keep up the good work."

Chapter 25
Foster Parent

During my spare time, I would often go fishing or play basketball and would sometimes take my neighbor's child, Craig, with me to the base to play ball at the gym. Craig and his family lived across the street from us, and I would often see the kids when they would come outside to play. They were a mixed family: The father was white, and the mother was black. They had four children: three boys and a girl. They seemed like a likable family. Craig was the average height of a fourteen-year-old, was mixed, and had curly hair. He had a baby face and looked younger than his age; he was a handsome young man with thick eyebrows.

They had been living across the street for three years before I met Craig. Craig would come over to the house, and he and I would have long conversations. Craig became comfortable with me and shared a lot about himself and his family. He shared with me that he and the other two boys were biological brothers and had been foster children before being adopted. The daughter was the biological child of the parents. Craig had been in the foster care system since he was five. His mother had given birth to him at fifteen, was strung out on drugs, and had been in jail since he was six. Since Craig's biological father wasn't around, there was no one to take care of him, and the state had to place him into the foster care system.

For the next four years, Craig lived in six different foster homes. At the age of nine, he was put into the care of my neighbors, who would adopt him at the age of eleven. Craig would share with me the troubles that he was having with his adoptive parents and how the situation at home was terrible. Craig is biracial and was placed into my neighbor's foster family specifically because they were a mixed couple and it seemed to be a good fit culturally. However, Craig liked to play sports and loved football and basketball. But Craig's adoptive father didn't like sports at all and didn't like it that his son did. He and Craig would get into arguments about Craig's hobbies. Craig was the oldest foster son. When the father would get upset with Craig, he and his wife would send Craig to the room that he shared with his brothers and tell him to color in his coloring books. I do not know any fourteen-year-old boys who want to color in coloring books.

The relationship between Craig and his adoptive parents had gotten so toxic that they were going to send him back into the foster care system. Craig's adoptive parents couldn't control him, and the police had been called to their house several times.

During one of our trips to the gym, Craig said to me, "Mr. Anthony, my adoptive parents are going to get rid of me."

"What do you mean *get rid of you*?" I questioned.

"They're going to send me back into the foster care system. Can you please adopt me? Please!"

This took me by surprise. After I picked my jaw up off the ground, I told him, "Craig, I am not sure that I can do that." I left the conversation alone. One Sunday afternoon, a week after Craig and I had that conversation about my adopting him, someone rang my doorbell. It was Craig's adoptive parents. I invited them in, and Wendy and I sat with them as they explained their situation with Craig and how they couldn't deal with him anymore.

"Craig is disrupting our household and the other children in it," The father said. They explained that Craig was on medication for attention deficit hyperactivity disorder and schizoaffective disorder.

They were aware of my relationship with Craig. The mother said, "Craig respects you. Would you and Wendy be willing to go through the process of getting the training and qualifications to become foster parents, so you could become Craig's foster parents?" The father added, "We don't want to put Craig back into the system, but we are at a point where we have no other choice." I told them that Wendy and I would discuss this and would let them know our decision; but before they walked out of the door, I asked them if they had sent Craig to his room to color.

"Yes," they said. "Every time he acts up."

That was all I needed to hear. We escorted them out, and I said to Wendy, "I believe that I could make a difference in Craig's life; he can relate to me. I'll take care of everything."

Wendy was reluctant and didn't want to take on the responsibility of caring for another child, especially one that wasn't her own.

"Craig would be my responsibility, and I would make sure that I didn't bother you for any assistance," I said. I felt compelled to try to help Craig because his whole life had been filled with turmoil, confusion, and pain but I understood my wife's hesitancy. It is a major responsibility.

Wendy finally agreed to let Craig live with us. But before that could happen, we would have to become foster parents. The next day I called Craig's foster parents and the social worker to inform them that we were willing to become foster parents. Craig's adoptive parents were so excited to hear the news and they immediately screamed as if they had won a prize.

The social worker said that normally both parents are required to go through the training and screening process to become foster parents, but since Craig's case was a special case, the requirements would be waived. I was able to become the foster parent and responsible party, but Wendy didn't have to sign up for that.

Wendy was glad because she was still reluctant to have Craig living with us because of his past. So, she did not want to go through the lengthy process of becoming a foster parent.

I didn't see this situation with Craig happening—it all took me by surprise. I did feel bad for Craig. I felt that he was acting out because he didn't have anyone in that house whom he could relate to. He hadn't really gotten to know his biological mother or father, had been in and out of foster homes, and was on medication. This was a lot for a child to deal with, and now he couldn't relate to the parents who had adopted him. Craig was a black kid at heart. Even though he was mixed he preferred black culture music and activities. He liked things that his adoptive father had no clue about and did not understand. Although the adoptive mother was black, she seemed as if she couldn't understand why Craig would rather listen to rap and R&B music than the Beach Boys or Tom Jones.

To become a foster parent, I had to verify my income, provide a physician's report verifying that I was physically and mentally capable of caring for a child, and submit to a National Fingerprint Criminal Record Check, a child abuse and neglect history check, and a DMV check. I also had to attend three face-to-face interviews, complete a home study, provide three references, complete pre-service training, after attending a one-time orientation to learn what foster parenting was all about.

There was a lot that I had to accomplish before becoming a foster parent.

I was clearly all in and wanted to be the best foster parent that I could be. Since Craig was a special case, I was able to get my paperwork processed quicker than I might have otherwise; and after a month, I was able to take custody of Craig. When I went to my neighbor's house to tell them that I was qualified and had been approved by the state to care for Craig, they couldn't hide their smiles. Did they know something that I didn't?

Craig moved into our house a week later, in August. He was the happiest kid that I had seen in a long time. We gave him his own room. He'd had to share with his two brothers before.

Tony wasn't living with us at the time, and when I told him about becoming a foster parent to Craig, he wasn't happy about it. "Dad, are you sure you want Craig living with you?"

"Why would you ask that?" I asked.

"Craig is a problem child, and I don't like him."

I told Tony, "Craig will be fine. He can't control me." But Tony knew Craig before moving out, and he didn't trust him. He thought he was a "big liar."

We treated Craig just like we treated our own son and showed him things that mattered the most: attention, kindness, respect, and love. I had to take Craig to see his doctor every month so that he could get his medication.

Craig was difficult at times, and Wendy didn't like that he continually lied to her. One day she told me Craig took twenty dollars out of her purse. "I had two twenty-dollar bills, and now I only have one," she said. "I know the money didn't just grow feet and walk away."

I asked Craig about the money, and he vehemently denied seeing or taking it. I left it alone and put it in the back of my mind. There would be other incidents that would suggest that he might be lying. I didn't want to believe that he was stealing or lying to us since we had provided everything for him.

It got to a point that my wife didn't feel comfortable with him in the house. We would catch him watching porn on the internet, and he would lie and say that he wasn't. I would then look at his computer's search history and find countless porn sites that he'd visited. I knew that he was almost fifteen and his hormones were raging, but I didn't appreciate him lying to me. It seemed worse that when Craig got caught lying red-handed, he would double down and continue to deny it.

The rift between Wendy and Craig continued to grow. One day, my gold chain and pendant came up missing from our jewelry box. I knew they were in that jewelry box because they were always there when I wasn't wearing them. I gave Craig the benefit of the doubt and searched my entire house looking for the jewelry, hoping that I would find it but knowing at the same time that it was gone. I received a call the next day from Craig's school. It was the guidance counselor informing me that Craig had on some jewelry. When they asked him about it, he couldn't explain where he had gotten it, and they figured that he might have taken it from home. They were right. When I went up to the school and I saw Craig, I think my blood pressure must have risen high as hell. I was able to get my chain back, but apparently Craig had given my pendant to someone and could not remember to whom he'd given it to.

Two weeks later, Craig and I were on base at the Navy Exchange store doing some shopping for school supplies. After I paid for all the items, Craig and I were leaving the store when security stopped us and asked us to follow them to their office. I didn't know what was going on. Once in the office, they showed me the surveillance cameras, and I was able to view Craig placing miniature alcohol bottles and condoms into his pockets. After they made Craig remove the stolen items from his pocket, they told me that Craig was prohibited from coming on base. I was extremely embarrassed, frustrated, and disappointed, and I couldn't hide my anger.

The ride home was long and quiet as I gathered my thoughts and determined how to deal with what had transpired. When we got home, I spoke with Craig and conveyed to him the seriousness of stealing and told him it wouldn't be tolerated. He assured me that he wouldn't do it again, but that wouldn't be the last time he stole something. Craig had lived with us for six months, and it had reached a point where someone had to leave the house—either Craig or my wife. I had given Craig many chances to stop lying and stealing, but he wouldn't. So, even though I hated it, my only choice was clear, Craig had to go.

I was hurt when I had to call his social worker and tell her that we were sending him back. Craig cried and begged us to not send him away.

"Dad, please don't send me back. Please, please, please," he said while the tears streamed down his face. I had never seen anyone cry and beg like he did. It instantly confused me, and I immediately felt like I was letting him down. I knew that he needed me, but I could not provide the degree of help that Craig needed. I had never turned my back on anyone, and now I felt like I was betraying him.

When the social worker arrived and helped him load his belongings into the city van, Craig's tears and loud wailing were more than I could stand. It cut to the core of my heart. I felt helpless. As Craig and his social worker were driving away, I could see him staring at me through the window with tears in his eyes as he slowly waved goodbye.

Craig would stay in touch with me. I would be there for him to talk to, and I still provided some financial support at times. Even when he would find himself locked up in jail, I would put money on his book sometimes to help with his commissaries. But I didn't want him to think that he could keep getting into trouble and I would send him money. I knew that he didn't have anyone else in his life. He called me "Dad" and still does to this day.

At twenty-eight years old, he is no longer in jail. He has a job, his own apartment, a car, and a son. His biological mother is out of jail, and he is trying to build a relationship with her. In a lot of ways, I could relate to Craig and understand how he may have felt when he didn't have someone he could talk to or confide in. Craig had a difficult life from the beginning, and often children in his position end up dead or in jail. I am thankful that I didn't completely give up on him because he needed someone even after he left our home. I couldn't see myself turning my back on him. I knew that he had the potential to do better. His emotional, psychological, and physical issues requiring medication made matters worse. We still stay in touch with each other, and he knows that I never really left him.

Chapter 26
Cookout

James's wife convinced him to move their family to Atlanta, Georgia. The quality of life was better, and the cost of living was much lower than in New Jersey. So, they moved to Atlanta and purchased a beautiful five-bedroom, two-story home.

I hadn't spoken to my father since the first day that we met. I had tried reaching out to him several times, but he never returned any of my calls. All wasn't lost, as I had the telephone numbers for one of my brothers and all my sisters, and we stayed in touch. I would often visit my siblings when I went to Atlanta to visit my friend Leon and my brother James. I would ask my siblings about our father, and they would tell me that he was doing fine. I tried to visit him when I was in Atlanta, but he was never available. I was happy that I was building a good relationship with my siblings and that my father didn't matter.

Atlanta's cost of living was a lot lower than Virginia's, and the home prices there were ridiculously low. During one of my visits to Atlanta, I met with a realtor and was able to find a townhouse that Wendy and I could purchase. The home was built recently and was only four years old at the time. It was a two-story, brick-front townhouse with a one-car garage, three bedrooms, two and a half baths, an electric fireplace, and practically new appliances.

The custom-built home was almost in move-in condition, even though it was in foreclosure. I had to fix the water heater, paint the entire inside, and clean all the carpets before it was ready to rent out. My realtor was able to find tenants who met my rental requirements, and I was officially a landlord. I never envisioned being a landlord or being able to afford an extra home that I didn't live in. As a landlord, I was determined to not be like the landlords that my mother had to deal with when I was growing up in Brooklyn. They had only cared about receiving the rent and not ensuring that their tenants were provided for. They did no renovations or necessary maintenance. It was a great deal and I paid just $26,000 for the townhouse and was now renting it out for $900 a month. I could have charged more for rent, but I was eager to have tenants and didn't want the townhouse to be vacant too long since the neighborhood wasn't safe.

Finally, I felt it had been long enough—I decided to reach out to my father one last time. I had decided that if he didn't want to have anything to do with me, I'd be OK with that. I called him and we spoke. I told him the next time I came to Atlanta to check on the house, I would like to meet with him. He said, "Sure."

I hadn't established a relationship with my father, but it was a great feeling knowing that my siblings wanted me to be a part of their lives. I stayed in touch with brother Bob and sisters Kendall, Brenda, and Sarah. We would call each other often. It was odd at first building a relationship with family members after forty years. Bob would share with me that our father was never really a provider for him or our other siblings and how he didn't rely on our father for anything. I remember my sister, Kendall, telling me that she and my other siblings had spoken in the past about wanting to meet me, but as was the case with my father, they didn't know where I was.

Kendall didn't see our father much at all. "Is seems he was too busy making children," she said. "I felt neglected."

All those years, I was wondering about my father and his whereabouts: Would I ever see him? Did I have any siblings? I had so many more questions. Now I was finding out that my father wasn't even being an adequate father to the children who were near him. His separation from me, in some ways, was no different than his isolation from my siblings. They, too, were missing a father in many ways.

My sister, Sarah, loves the ground that my father walks on. "My father has always been in my life, and he's good to me," she said to me.

I am the oldest of both my mother's and father's children, so now I was a big brother to a lot more siblings. Later that year in July, Bob called and asked if my family and I could come to Georgia in September. They were going to have a big cookout for me, and all my family members would be there. Excited and nervous, I said, "Yes, I would love to."

For the next two months, I was anxious. I remember telling one of my coworkers that I was going to meet my family in Georgia. I remember him telling me, "Enjoy your new family because life is short."

"Yes, it is," I replied, determined to have a good time.

I called my mother and told her about my conversation with Bob, how they were having a cookout for me, and that all my family members would be there. My mother was planning to go to Atlanta to visit James and her grandchildren during the time of the cookout. So, I asked her if she would like to go. After asking, I immediately thought how awkward and strange that might be.

Syrup Sandwiches

There was a long pause as if she was giving it some serious thought. Then she said, "Sure."

I said, "But will you feel comfortable seeing my father? I'm quite sure he'll be there too." She was quiet again, this time for longer than I expected. "Are you still there?" I asked.

"I'm still here. I'll be OK," she said.

"OK, fine," I said. "Should I come get you and drive you to Atlanta, or would you rather take a bus or fly?"

I knew she wouldn't fly because she was terrified of flying. I would give her a hard time whenever she mentioned that she was afraid to fly especially when it was time for her to come visit me in Florida or Virginia. I would tell her not to be afraid, that God would take care of her. I guess my logic wasn't good enough for her. I knew she loved the Lord, but she didn't trust that he would keep her safe while flying. Go figure. She decided that she would rather take a bus to my brother James' house in Atlanta. I couldn't imagine why she loved traveling on a bus. They were usually crowded, and some of the people on the bus didn't have the best hygiene. Besides, the ride from New York to Atlanta would take sixteen hours. I supposed she liked riding on buses so that she could see the change in scenery as the bus travelled from state to state.

My mother arrived in Atlanta three days before Wendy and I did. My son was living in California at the time and could not make the trip to Atlanta. Wendy and I flew into Atlanta and would be staying with my best friend from the Navy, Leon, who was also living in Atlanta. After our flight landed, we took the tram to the car rental location, then drove to Leon's house. Leon and his family would also be attending the cookout. Leon had two girls and was in a common-law marriage with the mother of his children. The family had a big German shepherd that Wendy feared. Their dog, Cassie, loved me and I would take her on walks whenever I came to visit.

The day of the cookout, we headed to Sarah's house. She lived in Ellenwood, about twenty miles southeast of Atlanta. My sister had a pretty home and an enormous backyard, large enough to accommodate the large number of people expected at the cookout.

Wendy and I pulled up to the house. Leon and his family followed close behind. I saw my mother and James and what appeared to be about a hundred people. This wasn't a cookout—it was a family reunion. There were so many people there, and I didn't know anyone other than some of my siblings whom I had seen during my previous visits. I felt lost, scanning the crowd for familiar faces. My brother, Bob, came up to me and started introducing me and Wendy to person after person. My father was there, and so were five of the six women who had children by him, including my mother.

I met all my father's family, including uncles, aunts, cousins, nieces, and nephews. I was overwhelmed to meet so many family members—for them not to have been a part of my life for over forty years was surreal. It was exciting to meet everyone, but at the same time it was slightly depressing. I had so many emotions running through my mind.

I had missed so much of my siblings' lives, and they had missed many years of mine. Relationships can take years to build, and some of my elderly family members didn't have many years left. Building a relationship with them would probably never happen. I learned that my paternal grandfather had passed away four years earlier. My paternal grandmother, whom I had met back in 1986, had become frail. She was at home and unable to meet my family.

By the end of the day, I was physically drained from talking to, shaking hands with, and hugging so

Syrup Sandwiches

many people. I wasn't used to all that attention. Now that I had met all the family that I hadn't known for most of my life, I had a lot of catching up to do. I made sure that Wendy and I went to visit my grandmother the next day and spent some quality time with her. I promised myself that I would visit my grandmother, brothers, and sisters as often as possible.

I finally got the opportunity to talk with my father alone. Before I'd met him, I wanted to not like him, maybe even hate him. But after hearing his side of the story and realizing that he didn't know how to be a caring and loving father, I was less angry. I still had questions for him: I questioned why he wasn't there for all his kids. My father didn't have any good answers, and I will have to live without fully understanding him. Still, I have found some closure and realize that sometimes people aren't sure why they do or say things. You can either accept or ignore what you can't understand.

My father was young when he started having children. I believe that he, too, lacked the fathering that he needed to ensure that he was sufficiently prepared to be the father that he should have been. It was clearly a cycle of bad fathering passed down on my father's and my mother's side. That cycle of bad parenting ended with me. I believe that if you are aware of a problem that affects you, and you do nothing to rectify it, you are in some ways complicit to your own detriment.

Over the next four years, I would take many trips to Atlanta to visit my grandmother and siblings. I would enjoy sitting and speaking with my grandmother and listening to her talk. She was mainly confined to the bed, but her mind was still sharp. It felt good to have a grandparent whom I was able to bond with. I needed that. She gave me the love that my heart was missing. I was in sync with her emotionally. Seeing her unable to move as she wanted made me feel miserable, not only for her but for me too, as there was nothing that I could do to make her situation better. I do know that she enjoyed seeing me. Her eyes would open wide, and she would have an enormous smile when I walked into the room.

  I had spent many years wondering about my dad and his family. I was thankful for the opportunity to get to know some of my relatives that I did not know as a child and build relationships with them.

Chapter 27
More Poor Decisions

In the fall, I graduated from Saint Leo University with a bachelor's degree in sociology. It was a long journey, and I had finally achieved something that I used to think was unachievable. The graduation ceremony was held at the historically black Hampton University in Virginia at its convocation center. There were probably about 4,000 people in attendance. This was my second graduation. My first was from high school many years ago, and there may have been maybe 300 people there. But this was totally different. There was a band and countless guest speakers. The ceremony lasted three hours. By the time they got to my name, I was more than ready for them to call my name so that we could go home. My wife and son were there, along with James and Leon, who had come from Atlanta for the ceremony. After the ceremony, we went home and had a cookout to celebrate my accomplishment.

I now had my eyes set on getting my master's degree. Three years later, I would receive my Master of Business Administration in December from Saint Leo University. The graduation ceremony was held at the same location as the graduation for my bachelor's. It was like déjà vu, only this time I really felt like I had achieved something special. I had more friends and family attend this graduation than the last one. I even had a friend stay at my house during the ceremony and prepare all the food so that I wouldn't have to do it, which was a tremendous help and relieved a lot of stress.

Shortly after my graduation, James informed me that he and his wife were getting divorced and that their house was in foreclosure. Then I learned that the realtor who was managing my Atlanta townhouse had been unable to collect rent from my tenants. The tenants, who were three months behind, would eventually move out without paying the rent and would leave the house in terrible condition, leaving clothing and garbage through the entire house.

It was June 19th, when Bob called and told me that our grandmother had died. I was so disconsolate after receiving the news that I hung up the phone and cried, thinking *why did I have to experience so much loss in my life?* I had to call Bob back to get the burial information, and he asked if I would be there.

"Of course, I will be there," I said. "She's my grandmother, too."

Wendy was unable to attend the funeral, so I flew to Atlanta and stayed at Leon's house. He and I went to the funeral together.

The funeral was on an extremely hot day. The service was held in a good-sized church, not like the tiny church that held the services for my other relatives. This church had room for hundreds of people and room for a piano, so I expected it would have good air conditioning. I didn't know that my grandmother was a Jehovah's Witness. Their burial services are totally different than what I was used to. The service was so long and dry that everyone was looking at each other and trying to figure out if this service would ever end as it got hotter and hotter in the church. I guess the air conditioner didn't work, or they were trying to save some money. Either way, it was miserable sitting there almost drenched, listening to everyone who spoke act as if time wasn't a real thing.

Syrup Sandwiches

I was scheduled to fly back to Virginia shortly after the service ended, and I kept looking at my watch to keep up with the time so as not to miss my flight. When it was finally over, I went up to the casket, gave my grandmother a kiss on her forehead, and said, "I love you. Rest in peace." Then I headed back to the airport.

I went back to Atlanta in September of that year to have the house professionally cleaned and painted. I then rented the house to my brother, James, and his four girls. James and his children moved into my townhome that winter. They adjusted quickly to the smaller home, considering they had been accustomed to a much larger house. James and his children were happy.

Finally, everything was going well in the family again—that was, until my sister Rhonda from Brooklyn called and needed my help. She had given up the apartment and job that she had in Brooklyn so that she and her two boys could move to Pennsylvania. One of Rhonda's sons had a girlfriend whose mother promised her a job, prompting the move to Pennsylvania. Rhonda gave up the apartment that she and my mother had shared until my mother moved out and into a seniors' apartment complex. Rhonda quit her job and moved with her two sons to Pennsylvania, giving up the low-income apartment that she and my mother had lived in for over two decades. My sister got the job that she was promised at a factory in Pennsylvania, but a month later she was laid off and needed help with her rent. Wendy and I helped her pay her rent, and after a month, she was rehired. I thought that everything was fine, but that was temporary. Two months later she was laid off again—at the same time that her landlord served her an eviction notice. She had no job and was about to be evicted. She called me, and I was compelled to assist. She and the boys needed a place to live, so I called James and asked him if the boys could come down and live with him in

Atlanta until Rhonda got situated. I told James that I would reduce the rent to half if he would allow the boys to come and live with him until Rhonda could get back on her feet. The boys were sixteen and twenty years old. James agreed to let the boys move in with him. But Rhonda was, for all intents and purposes, homeless. She couldn't stay with our mother because she lived in a senior-living community. She couldn't live with Wendy and me because she didn't drive and would certainly need a car to get around in Virginia. Nor could she move to Georgia with James and her boys for the same reason.

I contacted my Aunt Lillie and explained the situation that Rhonda was going through. Aunt Lillie was reluctant to allow Rhonda to come and live with her. She said, "Rhonda doesn't communicate or stay in touch with me. I never hear from her."

I knew that I was asking a lot from my aunt because she was right, Rhonda didn't call or visit her. How could I expect her to open her home to someone that she was related to but barely knew?

My aunt finally relented saying, "Anthony, I am going to do it, but I am only doing this because you asked me to."

I thanked my aunt and told her how much I loved her. Relieved, I contacted Rhonda and told her the good news. I helped Rhonda move from Pennsylvania to Manhattan. Luckily, she was able to get her old job back as a security guard.

Three years later, Rhonda was finally able to get some resemblance of her old life back. She was now financially in a better position, had gotten an apartment in New Jersey, and was able to move out of my Aunt Lillie's apartment. My nephews had lived with James for three years, and the youngest had graduated from high school with plans to possibly join the military. The oldest son was thinking about going to Job Corps to learn a trade and to get his Graduate Equivalency Degree (GED). James and I had everything set up for the boys to start their careers.

When Rhonda found out that her sons would be pursuing jobs and furthering their education, she immediately told her sons that the military and Job Corps were dangerous, and she didn't want them to go to either of them. She contacted James and me and told us, "I'm going to Atlanta to get my boys."

We pleaded with her, telling her that everything would be fine and that the boys would be OK. But she refused to listen to our sound advice and chose to go to Georgia and move her boys back to New Jersey with her. She and her boys, along with their belongings, took the long Greyhound bus ride from Atlanta to New Jersey.

James and I were frustrated not only with Rhonda for her complete selfishness but with her sons for not standing up for themselves and letting their mother know that they were not little boys anymore and no longer wanted to be under their mother's thumb. They were nineteen and twenty-three when Rhonda came and got them. At twenty-five and twenty-nine, they were still living with her in a two-bedroom apartment, and neither of them had jobs. When I get the opportunity to speak with Rhonda, she avoids any conversation about her sons. Growing up without any male guidance, James and I thought that we would be there for the boys to provide for them a level of male support that we didn't have. I will remain available to my nephews to impart any knowledge, support, or guidance they may require. Maybe one day they will take advantage of my gained experiences.

Chapter 28
Big Brother

Now that I had accomplished all that I wanted in terms of education, I needed something to keep me busy, but I wanted it to be something rewarding. I decided that I would research being a Big Brother. I discussed my decision with Wendy, and she was not too keen on the idea. She reminded me about how the situation with Craig turned out.

"Anthony, I hope this isn't another Craig problem."

"This is different. There are children who need someone in their lives to help them develop and teach them things. They won't live with us," I said.

I thought about how James and I grew up with no male role models, no mentors, no fathers, and no one who gave a damn. Now I could make a difference and help a child who has been in a similar situation to what I was born into and deserved better. My effort was bigger than myself. I truly wanted to give back. I had come a long way from the life I had in Brooklyn, and I wanted to share what I'd learned. I missed a lot of years with my son while he was growing up and volunteering my time would allow me the opportunity to share some quality time with a deserving child. I could do a lot of the things with this child that I should have done with my own son. I have matured and learned over the years how to be an effective and caring parent. I took a lot of missteps before I got it right, and no matter how much I learn, I know I can continue to grow and mature.

Big Brothers Big Sisters of America is a formal, community-based mentoring program. This program pairs children with adult volunteers who are usually college graduates. The children are between the ages of six and eighteen and often come from low-income families that have single parents.

I met all the initial qualifications except the age requirements of being between twenty and thirty-four years of age. I was already fifty-one years old. Still, I felt that I had so much to offer; I applied anyway. The nearest chapter was located on the peninsula thirty-five miles away from my home. I would have to join that chapter as it was the closest to me.

Over 1,000 parents had applied for a mentor for their children. There was a shortage of volunteers on the peninsula, so the director allowed me to sign up as a mentor with the understanding that, if after a year I had met all the qualifications, they would consider extending my involvement with the program. I was screened by a Big Brothers Big Sisters caseworker during a personal interview. I had a home visit, a criminal, background, and reference checks to ensure that my involvement with the program posed no safety risks to the children.

All my paperwork came back without a glitch, and I was accepted into the program. Before a match could be completed, I had to meet with the youth and parent. My potential mentee was a bright little seven-year-old boy named Andrew. Andrew was dark skinned like I am and had a low fade haircut. His dark brown eyes accentuated his small face and electric smile. When I met him and his mother, Andrew was all smiles and was awestruck at my height. I towered over his four-and-a-half-foot, slim frame. Before we were matched up, his mother had to approve. She did so quickly, and I was now officially a Big Brother mentor. As a mentor, I had to meet with Andrew between two and four times a month for a year and we had to engage in the activities he chose. The meetings would last between three and four hours each time. That would be easy for me since I would have a lot of free time now that I was not studying for college exams.

Andrew was inquisitive and would ask questions all the time, which I expected. He wanted to know things like how old I was and if I would teach him to drive. He also wanted to go to the movies. One time, I took Andrew to see *The Lego Movie*. He was transfixed by the giant movie screen as we sat and ate popcorn, intently eyeing the movements of every character. Although I was only required to spend time with Andrew between two and four times a month, I tried to meet with him every week and sometimes twice a week by adding a weekend day.

We had developed a wonderful relationship, and we both looked forward to seeing each other. I wanted Wendy to feel comfortable with Andrew and the fact that I was spending time with him. I arranged a meeting with Wendy, Andrew, his mother, and myself. I wanted my wife to see that I was in the program for all the right reasons and wanted to be as transparent as possible.

Since my passion is fishing, I made sure that I took Andrew fishing with me. We went to a fishing spot on base that had a forty-foot pier that was once used by small boats departing and entering the base. We both sat in the folding chairs that I had brought with us and enjoyed the beautiful weather. I had already shown Andrew the basics of fishing like casting, baiting the hook, and how to reel, and he learned quickly. He enjoyed it so much that he asked when we could do it again. I told him that we could do it again in two weeks because I had other places that I wanted to take him.

I started to notice that Andrew's attention span was short and that he would often get bored quickly even if it was something that he wanted to do. I had to be creative to keep him engaged.

There was a big auto show that was being held at the coliseum in Virginia Beach, and I was hoping that Andrew would like to see some of the new and antique cars that would be on display. I took him to the auto show, and to my surprise, Andrew was thrilled to see all the cars and other vehicles that were there. The car show was practically sold out when we went, and there were people everywhere. We walked from car to car looking inside of each, me admiring the details and designs of the vehicles while Andrew tried to sit in every car that he could. He would run and jump into one vehicle after another.

Then, someone bumped into me, and I turned around to see what happened. By the time I turned around to tell Andrew that we had to move on to the next vehicle, he was gone. He must have gotten out on the passenger side. My heart sank, and I began frantically searching for him.

I didn't want to panic, but I started thinking that I could go to jail for losing someone else's child or worse, maybe he was lost, or someone had kidnapped him. Not to mention, I would be on the news, and people would think that I was an irresponsible person. There must have been at least fifty vehicles in the coliseum, and I had searched at least twenty of them. I wasn't sure if I should tell the police that I had a missing child. I was nervous, afraid, and ashamed. Before I could call the police, I checked a white cargo van that was about thirty feet away, and inside, in the back, Andrew and two other boys were playing.

I was so relieved and angry at the same time. Right then that showed me the seriousness of what I was doing as the temporary guardian of someone else's child and how it could easily have gone amiss. I was unraveled and thought about terminating my role as mentor in the program. I thought long and hard about quitting but didn't want to be another man who had given up on Andrew.

One day, when I had been mentoring Andrew for over six months, I decided to bring him over to my house and let him play some video games. Andrew enjoyed himself. After we played games, I showed him how to start a grill and how to cook on it. He was so excited that he asked me to take a picture of him holding the cooking utensils while standing near the grill. He wanted his mother to see the picture of him pretending to cook. I knew that having a Big Brother would be rewarding for Andrew, but I didn't realize how rewarding it would be for me as well. Being a mentor allowed me to become more patient, and it showed me how to slow down, relax, and enjoy life. Mentoring Andrew enriched my psyche because it allowed me to realize that I should be focusing on things that were important to me and not expending energy on things that were counterproductive and detrimental to my happiness.

I saw how my interaction in someone else's life had made a difference. I also saw that kindness, thoughtfulness, caring, and compassion are things most people desire, and that the need to feel valued and appreciated is universal. Andrew and I were driving back to his mother's house when he asked me a question I had never expected to hear.

"Mr. Anthony, why doesn't my father come over to visit me?" I felt like someone had punched me in my gut. I paused for a long time before answering his.

Finally, I said, "Andrew, some people are busy working and have hard jobs; and by the time they get home, they are so tired that all they can do is go to bed and sleep. I think that maybe your father is busy, and as soon as he gets a chance to come see you, he will."

Andrew didn't say anything for a while. He was probably saying to himself, "That's some bullshit, Mr. Anthony."

Finally, he said, "My mother said that he doesn't have a job."

"Andrew, not all men are the same," I said. "Maybe your father is the kind of man that doesn't know how to be a good father to his children. Maybe he still needs to learn how to grow up and treat you like he should."

"I hope he grows up soon," Andrew said. I didn't expect to have a conversation like that with a seven-year-old child. This conversation solidified in my mind the impact that fathers have on their children and how the absence of a father can have far-reaching consequences for the child at many stages of their life.

It was time to go fishing again, and like the last time, both Andrew and I looked forward to going. When we got to the base, we took all our supplies out of the car and headed to the boat ramp. We were catching fish left and right. It was great; he was happy and so was I. This was our fourth time fishing, and Andrew had gotten much better at it. As I was baiting my hook, Andrew kept walking toward the side of the pier. Before I could say a word, he walked right off the pier. I dropped everything in my hand and reached my long arms over the side of the pier and was able to grab him and pull him out of the cold water to safety. Luckily, the pier was only two feet above the water. Andrew didn't seem as rattled as I was. I was trembling with fear. I once again thought that I could have been responsible for losing a precious life.

We would meet for two more months before my one-year mentorship came to end. The director of the program informed me that Andrew wasn't eligible for the program anymore because the mother hadn't disclosed that he was on medication for attention deficit issues when Andrew was first enrolled in the program. I learned that was a violation of the program's requirement to list all medication prescribed for the potential mentee. I was disappointed that Andrew would no longer be in the program. The director also told me that they were no longer allowing volunteers into the program if they didn't live on the peninsula. So, after just one year I, too, was out of the program.

I am thankful that I was given the opportunity to share my experience, knowledge, and time with someone who was growing up in a similar situation as I. To this day, Andrew and I stay in touch. He is fourteen now and doing great in school. He is growing up fast.

Chapter 29
Pain in the Neck

After the Big Brother program, I decided to relax, do more fishing, and to improve my swimming skills at the YMCA. One day while swimming, my arms and legs became numb. I struggled to make it to the side of the pool. When I finally regained enough strength to exit the pool, I couldn't maintain my balance. I staggered to a nearby bench and sat down. I attempted to leave the pool area but couldn't stabilize myself.

It would be an hour before I was able to walk. I immediately called my doctor, and I was able to schedule an appointment for the following day. I knew something had to be wrong.

When I arrived at my doctor's office the next day, I was informed that my primary care doctor was not available and that I'd need to see another doctor. He examined me and told me that it was just anxiety from being in the pool. I explained to the doctor that it couldn't be—I had been in the pool many times. He stuck with his diagnosis.

Two days later, I was back at the pool again swimming, and the same thing happened. Both my arms and legs went numb. I went to the emergency room this time and left with a referral to a neurosurgeon. I was told that my nerve was pinched against my spinal cord. An MRI confirmed the diagnosis. I would have to have spinal surgery. I was told that they would have to cut open the back of my neck. I would need a laminectomy and fusion at C2–T1. That was all Greek to me, but it didn't sound good. I learned that laminectomy is also called *decompression surgery*. It's a surgical procedure designed to provide space around the spinal canal, relieving pressure to the spinal cord or nerves and the pain created by it, via removal of the back portions of the compressing vertebrae.

The spinal fusion would be done to help stabilize the sections of the spine treated with decompression laminectomy. The surgery would take about eight hours, and I would have rods, screws, and plates in my neck. My brain could not handle everything that the surgeon was telling me, and all I could do was put my face into my hands and cry. I had never been this afraid as an adult in my life, and the thought of having my neck cut open was unimaginable. I got a second opinion, and that doctor confirmed the first diagnosis. I had to have the surgery or risk becoming paralyzed from the neck down. The surgeon warned me that the surgery was risky—I could die on the table, become paralyzed from the neck down, or I could be fine. If the surgery was a success, I would have limited mobility in my neck and wouldn't be able to do a lot of the things that I once had. I thought to myself that these are not the best outcomes, not exactly what I had hoped for. I started feeling bad for myself, and I was scared.

I'd had many orthopedic surgeries on other parts of my body in the past including my fingers, shoulders, knees, and feet. They were all outpatient, and I recovered well. All my previous surgeries were due to sports-related ailments and injuries. This neck surgery was different. My other surgeries were bunts, but this would be a grand slam. I would be in the hospital for at least four days IF I lived. I couldn't imagine losing control of my own life. I felt like I would be giving complete control to the surgeons, and the thought of not having control started to depress me. Up until this point, I felt as if I had control of my life. Now, I didn't.

On the scheduled day, Wendy and I arrived at the hospital for my surgery. After the eight-hour procedure, I was wheeled out of the operating room and welcomed by my wife, son, and best friend, Leon, who had driven all the way from Atlanta to be there for me. In between my grogginess, I remember saying, "I'm alive!" and giving everyone nearby high fives."

However, my celebration was short-lived. By the next morning, I was in the most pain imaginable and couldn't move my neck. My head was hurting on both sides near my temples. I asked the doctor about the pain, and he told me, "We had to drill holes into your head to keep the halo in place during the surgery."

Damn. I was told to expect to be out of work for at least two months and that the healing process would be slow. I wouldn't be able to tilt my head all the way back, and my neck movement from left to right would be limited. *No more roller-coaster rides or physical sports,* I thought. I would often feel sorry for myself, but then I would think about the people who were less fortunate—those missing an extremity, or diagnosed with cancer, or any other diseases from a long list. I told myself to *man up and stop being a wimp.* My self-generated pep talks often worked, and it was then that I realized how blessed I was. I realized how helpful it was that I had to learn to be a parent to myself. The difficulties I had endured as a child had taught me resilience and the value of not giving up. Now, I would choose not to give in to despair and discouragement in my current situation.

Chapter 30
A New Birth

It has been five years since my neck surgery, and time has gone by extremely fast. Tony is now married to his lovely wife, Kate, from Guildford, England. And Wendy and I are now grandparents. My granddaughter, Billie, is my pride and joy. I get to spend quality time with her and have been able to be there to see her grow and take her first steps. I get a chance to do a lot of the things that I could not do for Tony when he was a baby. I believe that God has allowed Billie to be a part of my life to afford me the opportunity to make up for all that I missed in Tony's earlier life.

As I reflect on my life and where it started, how it transitioned up to now, I've learned that giving up is the easy way out—never give up. Having to do without the things we needed many times while I was growing up has taught me that perseverance, determination, and having the will to succeed will eclipse quitting and giving up. All the difficult experiences that my family and I had to endure taught me how to be responsible, dependable, resilient, and most of all, how to understand that life can be difficult but even more so if you make poor choices.

Most of the men in my family made many poor decisions that complicated their own lives and affected the healthy development of their children. Because they failed to step up as caring fathers, they compounded the problems their children faced, and they missed out on opportunities to provide love and guidance that their children needed from them.

I am thankful to the men in my family for teaching me, unbeknownst to them, the importance of fatherhood. The presence, or the absence, of a good father makes a tremendous difference in the decisions and direction of the family's next generation.

When my aunt told me to "Never give up even when it seems like the world isn't going to change," I did not realize how valuable that advice would be. When I was faced with racism and discrimination, I did not give up. Sure, it affected me emotionally and confused me, but I could not let it consume me or allow it to subjugate my character, because I knew that "this too shall pass." I had learned that life isn't fair, but I did not have to let that defeat me. Following my aunt's advice, I did not give up and let life beat me down. Rather, I continued to strive for success in an effort to change the world that would not change on its own. I knew then and now that some people are cruel, unforgiving, and deceitful but I also know there are wonderful people of all races that are caring, loving, and considerate.

Growing up fatherless can be difficult, and emotionally challenging. It is unfortunate that many have and will continue to be in the same situation. I could not wallow in my thoughts of not having a father, it was too draining and depressing. Once I realized that fatherlessness did not reflect or define who I could become, I was able to better understand and accept the separation. I did not permit my father's absence to erode my self-worth and thanked my mother for being strong and supportive.

I did not grow up thinking that I would be bullied in school, but it happened. At first, I thought that maybe it was me and that I was doing something to cause the bullying. I was quiet and kept to myself, and now that I am looking back on it, my quietness may have been an invitation to be bullied. However, there is never a good reason for anyone to be bullied. When it started happening, I felt afraid and alone and did not know how to deal with it. There was no one that I could talk to about it, I sure wasn't going to tell my mother and stress her out, so I dealt with it the best way that I could. I fought back. I had to fight to not be bullied. I had more fights in high school than I could have ever imagined.

It saddens me to this day that so many people are faced with the issue of bullying, and like me, must deal with it on their own. I had to convince myself that I was not the cause of the bullying and that I needed to stand up for myself. Having someone to talk with would have allowed me to feel as if I had some measure of support. Being bullied is not fun and no one should have to go through it alone. I would encourage everyone to speak out, talk to someone that you trust and make them aware of what you're going through. And you as adult, cannot turn a blind eye with the thought that it is just a kid thing. Take a stand! Demand respect for every child. Enforce consequences for those who bully others and seek help for the bully. Chances are the bully probably has some unresolved issues that are triggering their behavior.

Growing up hungry as a child was depressing. My decision to start working at an early age was hastened by the many hungry days and nights. I could not continue to allow my struggling mother to be overwhelmed, I had to help. While I missed out on a lot of free time as a child, I am sure that it kept me out of trouble and prevented me from falling in with the wrong peer group. It also taught me that my actions could make a difference in my situation. If I worked hard, things would improve for me. Looking back now, I would not have done anything different.

The church provided a level of tranquility for me and my family. It was a reprieve from the everyday stress, despair, and sadness. I am grateful that the church helps us develop the mental fortitude to endure our challenging life. Being involved in a community church provided a feeling of inclusion. Sure, I did not always understand the message from the preacher, but it was rewarding watching the adults welcome the sermons and with ecstatic enthusiasm. It was in church where I found acceptance and learned to respect others. I realized that I was not better than anyone, nor was anyone better than me.

As a child, you could say I was a victim. The trauma that I experienced resulted from the actions of others. From bullying and racism to an absentee father and witnessing violence, many things in my life could have resulted in insurmountable obstacles. Yet, even as a child, somehow, I knew that the way to get out of the life that I did not want and I did not create, would be up to me. I could spend my time blaming my father and the others who made my life difficult and embracing a victim's mentality, or I could refuse to be defeated. It wasn't fair and it wasn't my fault. Yet, I was the only one who could change my life. It wouldn't be easy, and it wouldn't be fast, but I was determined I would succeed. I decided I would be the person who reversed the negative cycle. I've come to the realization that during my fragile emotional state, the things that helped me overcome the horrors were prayer, laughter, and the belief that I couldn't allow myself to succumb to the things that I could not control. I realized that all that I could do was rock and roll with each punch that life threw at me. And when it knocked me down, I knew that it was not time to throw in the towel, but rather, the time to get back up and prepare myself for the next battle.

-END-

About the Author

A native of Georgia, but growing up in Brooklyn, New York, Anthony Owens considers himself a Brooklynite. Anthony proudly served 20 years in active-duty service in the United States Navy, providing humanitarian aid to foreign countries and fighting in two wars. Anthony has a long list of distinguished military awards and decorations for his exemplary service to our country. With an MBA from Saint Leo University, he is a federal information technology specialist in Virginia. A provider and protector for his mother, siblings, his only son, his wife of thirty-eight years, and his granddaughter. Anthony has broken the cycle of poverty and fatherlessness in his family.

Made in the USA
Middletown, DE
26 March 2023